ALEISTER CROWLEY
The Nature of the Beast

Other Aquarian books by Colin Wilson

C. G. JUNG: Lord of the Underworld
G. I. GURDJIEFF: The War Against Sleep
The Strange Life of P. D. OUSPENSKY
RUDOLF STEINER: The Man and his Vision

ALEISTER CROWLEY
The Nature of the Beast

COLIN WILSON

Aquarian/Thorsons
An Imprint of HarperCollins*Publishers*

The Aquarian Press
An Imprint of HarperCollins*Publishers*
77–85 Fulham Palace Road,
Hammersmith, London W6 8JB

Published by The Aquarian Press 1987
9 10 8

© Colin Wilson 1987

Colin Wilson asserts the moral right to
be identified as the author of this work

A catalogue record for this book
is available from the British Library

ISBN 0 85030 541 1

Printed in Great Britain by
Mackays of Chatham PLC, Kent

Contents

Acknowledgements

THIS BOOK is heavily indebted to many friends: to Israel Regardie, Gerald and Angela Yorke, Roger Staples, Stephen Skinner, Neville Drury, Francis King, Dolores Ashcroft-Nowicki and Robert Turner, all of whom know far more about magic than I do. And, like all the previous writers on Crowley, I owe a major debt to my friend John Symonds; there is a tendency among modern Crowley disciples to denigrate *The Great Beast* for its attitude of genial scepticism; yet it is hard to imagine how it could ever be replaced as the standard biography. I also owe many insights to the books of Kenneth Grant, particularly to his *Typhonian trilogy*. Finally, I owe my wife a debt of gratitude for reading and correcting the typescript.

CW

One

Does Magic Work?

I WAS in my early twenties when I first heard the name of Aleister Crowley; it was not long after the publication of John Symonds' biography *The Great Beast*. A friend who had asked the Finchley public library to obtain the book for him was told indignantly that nothing would induce them to spend the ratepayer's money on such vicious rubbish; the library even declined to try and borrow a copy through the inter-loan system. I was intrigued; what had Crowley done that he should be regarded as an untouchable by a London librarian? So when I found a copy in the Holborn library, I read it straight through in a weekend. On the whole, I must admit, I found Crowley irritating; he made me think of Shaw's comment about Mrs Patrick Campbell: 'an ego like a raging tooth'. His life read like a moral fable on the dangers of exhibitionism.

One thing puzzled me: the attitude of the biographer to his subject. Symonds seems to take the sensible view that Crowley's magic was a lot of self-deceiving nonsense. How then should one understand the following passage:

Conjuring up Abra-Melin demons is a ticklish business. Crowley successfully raised them—'the lodge and the terrace', [he wrote], 'soon became peopled with shadowy shapes,'— but he was unable to control them, for Oriens, Paimon, Ariton, Amaimon and their hundred and eleven servitors escaped from the lodge, entered the house and wrought the following havoc: his coachman, hitherto a teetotaler, fell into *delirium tremens*; a clairvoyant whom he had brought from London returned there and became a prostitute; his housekeeper, unable to bear the eeriness of the place, vanished, and a madness settled upon one of the workmen employed on the estate and he tried to kill the noble Lord Boleskine [one of

Crowley's aliases.] Even the butcher down in the village came in for his quota of bad luck through Crowley's casually jotting down on one of his bills the names of two demons, viz. Elerion and Mabakiel, which mean respectively laughter and lamentation. Conjointly these two words signify 'unlooked for sorrow suddenly descending upon happiness'. In the butcher's case, alas, it was only too true, for while cutting up a joint for a customer he accidentally severed the femoral artery and promptly died.

Symonds' tone of light irony implies that he thinks this was all Crowley's imagination; in which case, what really *did* happen? And what really happened in that Cairo Hotel room on 8 April 1904, when a voice began to speak out of the air, and dictated to Crowley *The Book of the Law*? Symonds avoids the question with the comment: 'To enter, however, into the theological side of Crowleyanity is beyond the scope of this biography'.

Two or three years later, not long after the publication of my first book *The Outsider*, I came upon Charles Richard Cammell's book *Aleister Crowley, The Man, the Mage, the Poet* and, as I read this, I found it hard to believe that he and Symonds were talking about the same man. Cammell came across Crowley's poetry in the early 1930s, and immediately became convinced that Crowley was a poet of genius. When he read Crowley's autobiography, *The Confessions*, he had no doubt that it deserved to rank with Cellini, Rousseau, and Casanova. In London, Cammell was introduced to Crowley—who was now sixty—and they became friends. The friendship was cemented when Cammell went to dinner and ate one of Crowley's hottest curries—washed down with vodka—without turning a hair. Crowley had a sadistic sense of humour, and loved nothing more than to see his guests rush to the bathroom to wash down a mouthful of his curry with pints of cold water; when Cammell asked for a second helping and a refill of vodka, 'Crowley was conquered. . . He owned later that I had defeated him over that curry.'

Yet Cammell also seems to beg the question of Crowley's magical powers. Describing Crowley's conjuration of the Abra-Melin demons, he also quotes Crowley's own statement that the house became filled with shadowy shapes. But Cammell adds the interesting comment that he believes

Crowley's later bad luck—his lifetime of near-poverty and literary failure— was due to his breaking of the sacred oath he took in the Abra-Melin ritual—an oath to use his powers only for good and to submit himself to the divine will. 'To me Crowley appears thenceforth to have been a man accursed: he lost all sense of good and evil, he lost his love, his fortune, his honour, his magical powers, even in large part his poetic genius. . .'

Not long after reading Cammell's book I met him at the opening of a painting exhibition in Chelsea—a gentle, bearded man who was startled when I told him that I had recently acquired my own copy of his book from New York; he was unaware that it had been pirated. As we stood in the crowd, with glasses in hand, it was difficult to speak seriously about Crowley; but Cammell confirmed that he regarded Crowley as a great misunderstood genius, an 'outsider', and that he thought Symonds' book was little more than a gross libel. Cammell died not long after our meeting, so I had no chance to learn more about Crowley from him at first hand.

In the late 1960s, I wrote my own account of Crowley in a book called *The Occult*, and a year or two later, entered into correspondence with another Crowley disciple, Francis Israel Regardie. Regardie—who made himself a bad reputation among 'occultists' by publishing the secret rituals of the Golden Dawn society—also detested the Symonds biography and was not greatly pleased with my own chapter on Crowley. But when I read Regardie's book on Crowley, *The Eye in the Triangle*, I found it hard to understand his loyalty. Regardie had become a Crowley enthusiast in 1926, at the age of 19, when he read Crowley's classic on yoga *Book Four*, and wrote to Crowley; the result was an invitation to join Crowley in Paris as his secretary. Within a few months—as a result of the intervention of Regardie's sister—they were officially expelled from the country. Regardie finally drifted to London and joined the magical society of the Golden Dawn. After Crowley, he found this insipid and resigned, then hastened the collapse of the society by publishing their rituals. He began to write his own books on magic, heavily influenced by Jung. And when he sent one of these to Crowley, the master replied to the disciple with some sharp criticisms. Regardie admitted later that he should have accepted the rebukes;

instead, he wrote Crowley a silly letter beginning:

> Darling Alice [an insulting diminutive of Crowley's Christian name, and a sly reference to his bisexuality]. You really are a contemptible bitch. . .

Crowley made no reply, but circulated an anonymous letter about Regardie that seethed with venom:

> Israel Regudy was born in the neighbourhood of Mile End Road, in one of the vilest slums in London. . . Apart from his inferiority complex, he was found to be suffering from severe chronic constipation and measures were taken to cure him of this, and also his ingrained habit of onanism. The cure in the latter case was successful, but Regudy abused his freedom by going under some railway arches and acquiring an intractable gonorrhoea. . .

Regardie actually prints this letter in full in *The Eye in the Triangle*, and adds:

> It took me a long time to forgive him for this disgusting bit of self-projection. It is only within the last few years that my admiration for him as a great mystic has triumphed over my resentment and bitterness, enabling me to put aside my contempt for the nasty, petty, vicious louse that occasionally he was on the level of practical human relations. . .

So it seemed that, in spite of his indignation about Symonds' 'libel', Regardie was in basic agreement with its view of Crowley's character. And I have to confess that I found myself wondering whether Regardie's decision to 'forgive' Crowley was not simply a piece of opportunism. After all, there had been a Crowley revival in the 1960s; the Beatles had even included his portrait among their culture-heroes on the cover of their Sergeant Pepper record. Regardie set himself up as Crowley's chief American disciple, and republished many of his books, no doubt (since Crowley left no family) greatly to his own profit.

Now, as I began to read the Crowley works that were now being republished, I came to understand why Regardie and Cammell admired him so much. Crowley has a clear, logical intellect and he can write with Shavian clarity. The *Eight Lectures on Yoga*, for example, have a breezy vitality, and reveal a mind of remarkable range; he is as comfortable talking about science and mathematics as about mysticism and poetry. When he was in a 'magical retirement' in a cottage in New Hampshire in 1916, he had with him a copy of Shaw's *Androcles and the Lion*, whose long introduction on Christianity is one of Shaw's most important works. Crowley found he disagreed with much of it, and wrote a commentary on it called *The Gospel According to St Bernard Shaw*.[1] He wrote it without thought of publication, and it is one of the best commentaries on Shaw ever written. It has remarkable penetration—its criticisms of Shaw's socialism are practically unanswerable—and is full of Crowley's typical humour:

> There is no such thing as self-denial. Self-denial is merely the self-indulgence of self-denying people. There is an old, old story of an old, old woman, very benighted, who had not heard of Christianity till the Scripture reader came and read her the story of the Crucifixion, at which she wept copiously; but she soon dried her tears, remarking, 'After all, it was 'is 'obby.'

Works like these soon convinced me that Crowley was far more than a self-advertiser. But that still left the major question unanswered: What about the magic? Surely that *had* to be total nonsense?

On this matter I also found myself changing my opinion. In *The Occult*, I had taken it for granted that witchcraft was basically an absurd superstition. So, for example, when I presented the case of the North Berwick witches, executed in 1591 for raising a storm in which they tried to drown James I, I had no doubt that this was basically a case of hysteria and superstitious credulity. Yet elsewhere in the book, I accept evidence that African witch doctors can perform authentic 'magic'. My friend Negley Farson had described to me how he had seen witch doctors conjure rain out of a clear sky. Another friend, Martin Delany, described how the local Nigerian witch doctor assured his company that the torrential rain, which had lasted for five weeks, would stop for two hours for a garden party. The rain stopped immediately before the party was due to start, and the sun blazed out of a

1. Published in 1974 as *Crowley on Christ*, edited by Francis King.

clear sky; it started again immediately after the party finished.

Why should I have taken it for granted that Scottish witches would be unable to exercise control over the weather? In fact, there was strong evidence that the Berwick witches possessed real powers. There was a point during the examination when the king himself decided it was all superstitious nonsense; whereupon one of the chief accused, Agnes Sampson, whispered in his ear something he had said to his bride on her wedding night; no one but the king and his bride could have known about it. The king changed his mind about the witches. Another of the accused, John Fian, had been secretary to the Earl of Bothwell, who had a reputation as a dabbler in black magic; and Bothwell had good reason to intrigue against his cousin the king. When the king was sailing back from Norway with his bride, a tremendous storm had almost sunk the ship, and it was this storm that the witches had confessed to raising, with Fian's help. One writer on the case asserts that Fian's confession was forced upon him by the horrible torture of the boot, which crushed his leg; yet twenty-four hours later, Fian escaped and made his way home; clearly, he was not so badly injured... When I re-read the case, I had to admit that, if we once allow the supposition that the Berwick witches possessed the same powers as African witch doctors, then it *was* conceivable that they were guilty as charged—and as, indeed, they confessed.

But *how* could a 'witch' influence the weather? My own supposition—which, I have to admit, left me vaguely unsatisfied—was that it was some form of 'mind over matter.' Dr Rolf Alexander's book *The Power of the Mind*, has a series of photographs that purport to show how, on 12 September 1964, at Orillia, Ontario, Alexander concentrated on a group of clouds, and dissipated them within eight minutes; other clouds around remain unaffected. He used 'psychokinesis'— 'mind over matter.' But that, admittedly, is a long way from causing a full-scale storm.

Stories of Crowley's own powers suggest that his magic was also some hidden 'mind force.' His friend Oliver Marlow Wilkinson described how, when Crowley was in the room, a man began behaving like a dog—begged, barked, whined, and scratched at the door. Wilkinson's mother had seen Crowley cause another man to act like a dog. This, of course, sounds like some form of hypnosis. But the American writer William Seabrook has a story of how Crowley demonstrated his magical powers on Fifth Avenue. On a deserted stretch of pavement, Crowley fell into step behind a man and imitated his walk. Then, suddenly, Crowley buckled at the knees and squatted for a moment on his haunches; the man collapsed on to the pavement. As they helped him to his feet, he looked around in a puzzled manner for the banana skin.

This is clearly not hypnosis, but it sounds like some curious form of telepathy—of the establishment of a 'sympathy' between Crowley and his victim. In the 19th century, hypnotists were much intrigued by a phenomenon they called 'community of sensation.' When a good hypnotic subject was placed in a trance, he would wince if the hypnotist stuck a pin in his own hand, and snatch his hand away if the hypnotist held his own hand above a candle flame; he would smile if the hypnotist tasted sugar, and grimace if he tasted salt. It sounded as if Crowley was using some variant of this principle.

It can be seen that, like most members of the Society for Psychical Research, I was inclined to look for explanations of the 'paranormal' in terms of scientific principles that we do not yet understand. And one of my best efforts in this direction concerned that strange phenomenon known as the poltergeist, or rattling ghost. Poltergeists are one of the best-attested phenomena in the whole range of psychical research. Hundreds—probably thousands—of cases have been observed by trained observers. But the Society for Psychical Research soon noticed that in nearly every case, there is a child or an adolescent in the house, and that when this person is not present, the phenomena—dancing furniture, banging noises, objects flying through the air—stop happening. And Freud's theory of the unconscious mind provided a more-or-less scientific theory to explain the phenomena: that they are not the work of disembodied spirits, but of violent tensions in this unknown region of the mind. Jung coined the term 'exteriorisation phenomena' to describe it, and tells the story of how, when he was arguing with Freud about the 'occult', and Freud was being contemptuously sceptical, he—Jung—experienced a burning sensation in his diaphragm, and there was a sudden loud bang from the bookcase. Jung said: 'That is an example of exteriorization phenomena.' 'Bosh!' said Freud. 'It is not bosh, and to prove it, there will be another bang in a moment.' And a second loud detonation sounded in the bookcase. Freud was rather shaken. *If* Jung was correct in believing that he somehow caused the bangs, this seems to be a fairly conclusive proof that poltergeists are actually a mischievous aspect of the unconscious mind.

But that still fails to explain *how* the unconscious mind causes objects to fly through the air—or how the 'ghosts' can converse in a code of raps, or even through human-sounding voices. Parapsychologists refer to poltergeist phenomena as 'spontaneous psychokinesis', but this also begs the question. There is strong evidence that some gifted subjects can move tiny objects—such as postage stamps and compass needles— by concentrating on them, but they are hardly in the same class as the poltergeist, which has been known to move a Landrover for several hundred yards.

It was not until I began researching a book on the poltergeist that I engaged in a systematic study of poltergeist phenomena through the ages. One thing immediately became obvious: that when communication has been established with the 'entity', it invariably claims to be some kind of spirit. And Guy Playfair, who had spent many years studying poltergeists at first hand in Brazil, told me that he had no doubt that most poltergeists *are* spirits. On the day after speaking to him, I went to interview a family in Pontefract who had been 'haunted' by a highly destructive poltergeist— it had smashed every breakable object in the house—which claimed to be the ghost of a monk who had been hanged on a gallows at the spot. The more I studied this case, and others like it, the more I became convinced that Playfair was right. By the time I began to write *Poltergeist!* there was not a shred of doubt in my mind: poltergeists are exactly what they claim to be, disembodied spirits. I found this conclusion thoroughly embarrassing; I would far rather have clung to the more respectable 'spontaneous psychokinesis' theory. But honesty compelled me to admit that it simply fails to explain the facts as completely as the spirit theory.

Playfair's book about his researches in Brazil—*The Flying Cow*—brought another startling insight: that there is a connection between poltergeist phenomena and magic. In the first case he investigated, in Sao Paulo, a Portuguese family was being subjected to continual persecution by a poltergeist: oddly enough, it had followed them from house to house. There were no children in the family: the son and daughter were both adults. The poltergeist kept them awake at night, set bedding on fire, and soaked it with water. There was some evidence of black magic: a photograph stitched with thread had been found in the house. Playfair heard the bangs, and witnessed other phenomena—at one point, a wardrobe full of clothes was set on fire and would have burned the house down if it had not been discovered.

The family finally decided to call in a *candomblé* specialist (*candomblé* is a form of voodoo). This man told the family that they were being persecuted by black magic—the troubles were connected with the son's marriage. And after the performance of various magical rites, the poltergeist left.

Playfair learned that 'voodoo' magicians or witch doctors can summon poltergeists, and direct them to cause trouble to certain people, and his book contains many other examples of this practice. Witches have always, of course claimed to make use of spirits. If Playfair was right, then this was quite literally true.

I must admit that all this left me feeling rather shaken. I had been studying 'the occult' for more than ten years, and had never doubted for a moment that most of its mysteries can be explained in terms of the unknown powers of the human mind—telepathy, clairvoyance, psychokinesis, and so on. It was startling to suddenly be confronted with evidence for the existence of 'spirits.' I had never actually taken the position that there are no such things as spirits; but I had always assumed that, *if* they exist, they play only a small part in paranormal phenomena. Now I found myself obliged to recognize that they play a central part.

It was also at about this time that I discovered Max Freedom Long's book *The Secret Science Behind Miracles*—an off-putting title that does no justice to the contents of the book. During his years in Hawaii after the first world war, Long devoted himself to the study of the ancient native religion of the *kahunas*, the 'keepers of the secret'. He soon learned that stories about the 'death prayer' were not the superstitious absurdity he had at first assumed, and that even

European doctors admitted that when a patient was brought into hospital suffering from the 'death prayer', there was very little they could do for them. Long's researches left him in no doubt that the kahuna magicians made use of a form of voodoo which involved making use of 'spirits' to drain victims of their vital energies until they died. Long's chief mentor, Dr Brigham, had once succeeded in saving one of these intended victims, and in directing the 'death prayer' back at the witch doctor who was responsible; the result was the death of the witch doctor.

It sounded preposterous, yet the evidence was overwhelming. It all pointed in the same direction: that poltergeists are 'spirits' who are able to manifest themselves only by making use of the energy of human beings—usually those who are emotionally disturbed. They appear to be of extremely low intelligence and to behave like bored juvenile delinquents. And they seem perfectly happy to assist 'magicians' in creating mischief, since this is the kind of thing they enjoy anyway.

Not long after the book came out, I encountered an interesting case that confirmed my findings. A young married woman wrote to ask my advice about a disturbing series of events that had happened to her in Brazil. She began to suspect that her husband was being unfaithful to her with a native woman. And a woman who claimed to be a clairvoyant stopped her spontaneously in a street and told her that she had been bewitched. Life seemed to turn into a series of minor problems and obstacles. The relationship with her husband became worse and worse. One day, as she sat in the bath, her wedding ring began to slip from her finger. She watched it with astonishment. It was a fairly tight fit, yet it slipped down her finger as if it had suddenly become loose. Then it fell into the water. When she got out of the bath, she decided not to pull out the plug, in case she lost the ring; instead, she carefully bailed out the water with a saucepan. But when the bath was empty, there was no ring.

A few weeks later, convinced that her marriage was about to break up, she obeyed a sudden urge to go and see her husband at his place of work and make one final plea. It worked; their differences dissolved and they made up. Back at home, she felt exhausted and decided to have a bath, and while she was in the bath, she decided to wash her knickers. As she picked them up to squeeze out the soapy water, her wedding ring fell out of them. Her story, far more detailed than I have reported, left me in no doubt that she was another victim of voodoo, and that her rival was probably responsible for the 'spell'. It was an interesting example of what can be accomplished by magic.

This recognition may have placed me beyond the pale of respectable scientific investigators, but it had the advantage of unifying my own views on the paranormal. Modern shamans or witch doctors declare that their power comes from the dead, from spirits, and that they perform their 'magic' with the aid of spirits. Their only power is that of mediumship, the ability to place themselves in contact with spirits. Shamans and witches have made the same claim throughout the ages, although they often insist that the 'spirits' are not only those of the dead; there are also nature spirits, or elementals.

In 1926, Montague Summers—whom Richard Cammell introduced to Crowley—achieved overnight fame with a book called *The History of Witchcraft and Demonology*. It was an extremely scholarly book, part of a series on the history of civilization. What startled the reviewers was that Summers seemed to believe every word he wrote about the 'enormous wickedness' of witches and warlocks. H.G. Wells launched a vituperative attack on it in the *Sunday Express*. He could understand how a Catholic could believe in the reality of evil; but the notion that human beings could have intercourse with demonic forces evidently struck him as sheer intellectual perversity; he obviously thought Summers was either a charlatan or an idiot. When I first read the book, in my teens, I thought Summers had his tongue in his cheek. Now, as I re-read it, I could see how Summers could believe in witchcraft without in any way compromising his intellectual integrity. I could also see that when Summers wrote: 'Modern spiritualism is merely witchcraft revived', he was not all that far from the truth. Throughout the ages, shamans and witches have established contact with 'spirits', and tried to use them for their own purposes; the Elizabethan magician John Dee had no such talents himself, and used a 'scryer' (descryer, or one who sees), another name for a medium. During the age of reason, belief in witchcraft finally evaporated; by the mid-19th century, scientists were totally convinced that all forms of 'occultism' were a relic of the bad old days of superstition. Then the curious poltergeist phenomena in the home of the Fox sisters in New York state caused a nationwide sensation. All over America, people began holding seances and discovered that it was easy to get 'phenomena'. The 'spirits' ordered the Fox sisters to found a new religion called Spiritualism, and prophesied its success. Within a few years, it had established itself all over the world, and the scientists raged and uttered denunciations as this new wave of 'superstition' made thousands of converts. In fact, the pendulum was simply swinging back in the opposite direction, and the world was rediscovering the most ancient of religions: shamanism.

In Russia, a lively overweight girl named Helena Hahn began to see 'spirits' at an early age, and realised she was a natural medium. She made an unwise marriage at sixteen to a middle-aged man named Blavatsky, and left him almost immediately. As she wandered around Europe as a travelling companion to various ladies, the tidal wave of spiritualism came rolling across the Atlantic. Helena Blavatsky became a friend of one of the most remarkable mediums of all time, the young American Daniel Dunglas Home, who could cause tables to float up to the ceiling and wash his face in red hot coals. Helena realised that her own psychic powers could probably be used to her advantage in America, and landed in New York in 1873, at the age of forty-two. Success was slow to come, but four years later, she achieved overnight fame with a book called *Isis Unveiled*, which became a bestseller. She explained to her disciples that she had acquired her esoteric knowledge in Tibet, where she had been taught by 'secret masters'. These masters of wisdom were in charge of human evolution on earth, and they communicated with her nightly, and sometimes during the day, by causing notes to drop from the air. The society that Helena Blavatsky formed with the aid of her admirer, Colonel Olcott, was called the Theosophical Society, and was devoted to disseminating the wisdom of the Masters. The year after *Isis Unveiled*, Madame Blavatsky decided to move the Society to India, where it achieved considerable success. A book about her teachings—or rather, those of the Masters—called *Esoteric Buddhism* by A.P. Sinnett also became a bestseller, and spread the doctrine far and wide; there were soon branches of the Theosophical Society in every capital in Europe.

Madame Blavatsky's downfall came in 1884, when the newly-formed Society for Psychical Research sent a young investigator to India to study her claims. But Madame Blavatsky was absent when Richard Hodgson arrived, and he fell into the hands of her disaffected ex-housekeepers, the Coulombs, who soon convinced him that she was a fraud. To some extent, they may have been telling the truth; yet no one who studies the evidence can doubt that she was a genuine and very powerful medium. Hodgson's report denounced her. Many followers remained faithful, but thousands of others left the movement. Madame Blavatsky moved to London, where she spent the last few years of her life writing a vast work called *The Secret Doctrine*; she died at the age of sixty. Yet in spite of her tribulations, and the general view that she was an old charlatan, Helena Blavatsky exercised an enormous influence on her time. Theosophy arrived at exactly the right moment. By the second half of the 19th century, there was a deep and powerful craving for some new form of religion. Darwinism had caused a major spiritual crisis. Many clergymen were beset by 'doubts' and felt obliged to resign their livings. In *In Memoriam* Tennyson expresses the despair of the sensitive intellectual when faced with an apparently meaningless and Godless universe. There was a general feeling that science had deprived man of all hope, and that it was time for a backswing of the pendulum. So when, in 1883, A.P. Sinnett assured readers of *Esoteric Buddhism* that there really were 'secret masters' in Tibet, and that they possessed the wisdom of the ages, he accidentally touched that spring of almost morbid craving for new spiritual values. Moreover, Sinnett was no crank; he was the respectable editor of India's most respectable newspaper, the voice of the establishment. *Esoteric Buddism* was like the falling rock that starts a landslide. The poet W.B. Yeats read it, and was wildly excited. He handed it to his friend Charles Johnston, who immediately rushed to London to get permission to set up a Dublin branch of the Theosophical Society. And the same thing was happening in Paris, Berlin, Rome, Vienna. (In Vienna, a young man named Rudolf Steiner, who was also striving to create his own revolt against materialism, was impressed by the book although he thought the talk of 'secret masters' too materialistic.) For all her faults, and for all the chaotic obscurity of her major works, Madame Blavatsky provided something that thousands were searching for.

Four years after the publication of *Esoteric Buddhism* a London coroner named Dr Wynn Westcott somehow came into possession of an ancient-looking manuscript written in a cipher that looked like a mixture of ancient Greek and astrological symbols. Westcott was interested in Freemasonry and occultism. He cracked the cipher, and discovered that the manuscript contained five magical rituals. He asked his friend Samuel Liddell Mathers, an eccentric scholar, to help him expand the material so the rituals could be performed. He also, he claimed, found among the manuscript pages the address of a certain Fraulein Sprengel in Stuttgart. He wrote to her, and learned that the rituals were the property of a German occult group called *Die Goldene Dämmerung*—the Golden Dawn—and she authorised him to set up a London branch of this magical order. So, in 1888, the Hermetic Order of the Golden Dawn came into being in London. Its purpose was the traditional purpose of magic: to establish contact with 'higher spiritual realms' by means of magical ritual and disciplines. Like the Theosophical Society, it touched some chord of intellectual craving, and soon had branches in Edinburgh, Weston-super-Mare and Bradford. The influence of Madame Blavatsky may be gauged from its complete title: the Isis-Urania Temple of the Golden Dawn.

But there was another influence that was equally powerful: the magician of whom Crowley later believed he was a reincarnation: Eliphas Lévi, the author of *Dogma and Ritual of High Magic*. Lévi, whose real name was Alphonse Louis Constant, was a failed priest who became a left-wing journalist. Then Constant became the disciple of a strange Polish nobleman named Wronski who believed that he had discovered the ultimate secret of life: how to use the sense-impressions of a lifetime to create ultimate reality inside one's own head. Wronski's wife thought he was a god, and so must have been surprised when he died in 1853. But Constant had met him in the year before his death, and after cataloguing Wronski's manuscripts, he plunged into the study of occultism. And in

1855 and 1856 he published his two-volume work on 'high magic'. Like *Esoteric Buddism*, this also began with an assertion of a mysterious secret doctrine that had been passed down the ages, which is 'everywhere the same and everywhere carefully concealed.' In that romantic era, the book achieved a wide influence. The English novelist Bulwer Lytton was greatly impressed by Lévi, and portrayed him as the magician in his most famous story *The Haunted and the Haunters*. He was also fascinated by Levi's claim to have conjured up the shade of the magician Apollonius of Tyana through magic rituals. Lévi claimed that the spirit answered his questions telepathically, and caused his arm to become numb by touching it. Lévi died in 1875, two years before Madame Blavatsky was launched to fame by *Isis Unveiled*, but he was regarded as a kind of saint of the new occult movement. Modern readers of his books on magic will find them disappointing. His knowledge of magic was obviously far smaller than he would like us to believe; for example, he sets himself up as an expert on the Hebrew Kabbalah without knowing a word of Hebrew. In short, Lévi was a mixture of poet and charlatan, and his books owe more to imagination than to scholarship.

The reader who based his ideas of magic on Lévi's books might feel justified in assuming that it is all self-deception and wishful thinking. This would be premature. In fact, many anthropological works contain accounts of shamanistic magic that make it clear that it can and does work. There are, for example, innumerable accounts of fire-walking. In 1899, a New Zealand magistrate, Colonel Gudgeon, went to watch a Maori fire-walking ceremony, and felt apprehension when he was invited to join in. But the words 'I hand my *mana*, my power, over to you' had the effect of making his feet immune to the red hot cinders, and he experienced only a tingling sensation. Max Freedom Long's mentor Dr Brigham had less faith, and declined to walk on the hot lava in a volcano without wearing his heavy boots. In the few seconds it took him to run across the lava, the boots were burnt off his feet, the soles flapping loose. Yet the kahunas strolled across with only a few leaves on their feet.

The trick, it seems, lies in the mental preparation. George and Helen Sandwith, who described the fire-walking ceremony in Fiji, noted that the essential feature was that the firewalkers 'were charged with some unknown type of energy. . and ten days of ritual preparation were devoted to this.' This enabled them to walk across a fire-pit so hot that it could cause scorching at a distance of twelve feet. In the mid-1980s, fire-walking spiritual cults spread from America to Great Britain, and were featured on television; perfectly ordinary people demonstrated that it was possible to walk on hot coals. But here again, it was clear that the essential feature was the mental preparation beforehand—the meditation, and the creation of a mood of total self-confidence.

All this would seem to indicate that the human mind has unsuspected powers over the body, but that these powers must be *aroused* from the depths of the mind. Lévi prepared himself for his invocation of Apollonius of Tyana by observing a vegetarian diet for three weeks beforehand, and fasting completely for the last week; during this time he meditated constantly on Apollonius and held imaginary conversations with him. The result of such preparation and concentration is to arouse some deep, unified will-force in the unconscious mind: what Crowley was to call 'the true will'. One of Shaw's Ancients in *Back to Methuselah* says: 'The brain shall not fail when the will is in earnest.' It would seem that Shaw had stumbled upon one of the basic principles of ritual magic. Aleister Crowley would devote his life to the exploration and analysis of this secret.

Two

The Reluctant Christian

THROUGHOUT his life, Crowley had serious public relations problems; he was widely regarded as a warped and depraved exhibitionist. And this was not due, as in the case of so many 'outsiders', to the incomprehension of the general public. It was due to a silly, schoolboyish desire to cock a snook at Victorian morality. So, for example, the marginal notes to a 1906 essay contain harmless-looking Latin phrases like '*Adest Rosa Secreta Eros*' and '*Quid Umbratur In Mari*', the sole point of which is that their initial letters spell 'arse' and 'quim'; the initials of another sentence spell 'piss' and 'cunt.' But when this was read out in court in a libel case four years later— when a friend of Crowley's named Jones was trying to defend himself against a particularly nasty journalistic attack—it had the unfortunate effect of causing the verdict to go against Jones. The defence argument was that anyone who was a friend of Crowley's had no reputation to lose, and the jury agreed.

This lifelong craving to shock and outrage the respectable stemmed from the hidebound pietism of Crowley's family background. His mother and father were fanatical members of the sect of Plymouth Brethren, and the cornerstone of their religious convictions was a belief in hellfire. They believed that every word of the Bible was divinely inspired, and that the Day of Judgement would arrive in the fairly near future, destroying everyone but members of their own sect. Crowley later described his mother as 'a brainless bigot of the most narrow, logical and inhuman type'. The same seems to have applied to his father, Edward Crowley, except that he possessed a high degree of dominance and vitality, so that his son hero-worshipped him. Crowley's own opinion about his early years can be gathered from the title of the preface to his book *The World's Tragedy*: 'A Boyhood in Hell'.

The elder Crowley was a 'gentleman of leisure', having inherited a flourishing brewing business from his own father, also named Edward; the latter had set up a series of 'alehouses' for the sale of his own beer, as well as ham and cheese sandwiches, and they became immensely popular with city clerks in the 1850s. The family wealth is almost as important as the family bigotry in explaining Crowley's own rebellious and autocratic temperament. In spite of the pietism of his background he was thoroughly spoilt. 'I was taught to expect every possible luxury. Nothing was too good for me. . . When I came into my fortune [at twenty-one], I was utterly unprepared to use it with the most ordinary prudence, and all the inherent vices of my training had a perfect field day for their development.' The result, of course, was that he spent most of his later life in a poverty that he furiously resented; it accounts for the note of self-pity that runs through the nine hundred pages of his autobiography.

Edward Alexander Crowley—who later coined the name Aleister—was born on 12 October 1875, in Leamington Spa, Warwickshire. He comments typically: 'It has been remarked a strange coincidence that one small county should have given England her two greatest poets—for one must not forget Shakespeare.' And just in case the reader has never heard of Shakespeare, he adds his dates (1550–1616) in brackets, getting his birth date wrong for good measure.

When Crowley was six, the family moved from Leamington to Redhill, in Surrey. His comments about this period suggest that he was something of a snob and something of a bully. 'Aristocratic feelings were extremely strong', and he and his playmates, who played games in which they were aristocrats, used to lie in wait for what they called 'cads'—children from the local school—and bombard them with peas and arrows. He was so convinced of his privileged position as one of the 'masters' that he one day charged a navvy working in a pit and knocked him down, then bolted home. On another occasion he attacked an errand boy with an Alpenstock, and was alarmed when the boy pursued him back home, 'when, of course, the elders intervened'.

Crowley's father was also something of a bully. When a lady called at the house for a subscription in aid of soldiers, 'he browbeat and bullied her into tears'. But he seems to have had a redeeming sense of humour. He told one of his congregations that he would prefer to preach to drunkards rather than teetotalers, because abstainers might fail to recognize their need for Jesus. When someone pointed out that this opinion might have some connection with the fact that his money came from beer, he replied that he had been an abstainer for nineteen years, during which time he had shares in a brewery; now he drank alcohol, but his money was invested in a waterworks.

Crowley's father died when the boy was eleven. It was partly his own fault; cancer of the tongue was diagnosed, but for religious reasons, Crowley senior decided to treat the illness with some quack-form of electro-therapy. Away at boarding school, Crowley dreamed that his father had died, and later recalled some peculiar quality in the dream that made him take it seriously; years later, he had a similar dream on the death of his mother. It seems clear that, in spite of his aggressive 'normality', Crowley was basically psychic. Crowley's reaction to his father's death was to cease to be a model schoolboy, and to begin to misbehave at school.

His mother moved to London, to be near her brother, Tom Bond Bishop, 'a prominent figure in religious and philanthropic circles'. He seems to have been much the same kind of 'brainless bigot' as Crowley's mother, and inspired in the eleven year old boy a paroxysm of loathing which does much to explain his later attitude towards Christians and Christianity. He devotes a page to castigating him in the autobiography, a passage that tells us as much about Crowley's ability to hold grudges as about his uncle's stupidity. 'Perfidious and hypocritical. . . he was unctuous as Uriah Heep, and for the rest possessed the vices of Joseph Surface and Tartuffe; yet, being without the human weakness which make them possible, he was a more virtuous, and therefore a more odious villain.' What really enraged Crowley was that this uncle was a 'right man': 'He was inaccessible to doubt; he *knew* he was *right* on every point.' Crowley later asked him what a climber should do if his companion should fall, and the only way of saving his own life was to cut the rope. His uncle replied: 'God would never allow a man to be placed in such a position.'

Uncle Tom started the process of turning Crowley into a

rebel. A taste of injustice at school acted as a further catalyst. The school—in Cambridge—was run by Plymouth Brethren, and the headmaster encouraged tale-bearing. Some fellow pupil 'with insane taint' (Crowley always foams at the mouth when speaking of those who have done him down) told the headmaster that he had visited Crowley at home and found him drunk at the bottom of the stairs. Neither Crowley nor his mother was asked about this; the headmaster merely issued orders that Crowley was to be 'sent to Coventry'—that no master or boy should speak to him. For a term and a half he became totally solitary, with no idea of what he had done. Finally his health broke down and he had to be removed. Crowley's account of the school—of 'trials' of wrongdoers that began with long prayers, and of pupils being half-flogged to death—make it clear why he became such a good hater of evangelical Christians.

His health was so poor that it was predicted that he would never reach the age of twenty-one; so a doctor recommended a course of travelling around the country with a tutor. Crowley learned to climb mountains and fish for trout. The only drawback was that most of the tutors were chosen by Uncle Tom, and were of the 'sawny [Scottish], anaemic, priggish type.' 'Of course, I considered it my duty to outwit them in every possible way and hunt up some kind of sin.' One of them, the Rev. Fothergill, even tried to drown him after Crowley had thrown him out of a boat. And it seems to have been immediately after this that Crowley succeeded in hunting up his favourite kind of sin. 'That night the gods still further favoured me, for a village girl named Belle McKay found herself with nothing better to do than to roam with me amid the heather. We returned together quite openly and Fothergill threw up the sponge. He took me back to London the next morning. Breaking the journey at Carlisle, I repeated my victory with a buxom chambermaid.'

Crowley's next tutor, the brother of the Dean of Westminster, did his best to seduce him. Crowley resisted—not, he admits, out of lack of inclination, but because he thought it was a trap to betray him to his family. The tutor later apologised to Crowley, explaining that he had been led into evil ways by his elder brother, a missionary. Crowley loves to tell this kind of story—the reader can almost hear him chortling and rubbing his hands. Like de Sade, he would love to believe that every clergyman is a secret pervert.

Subsequently, Uncle Tom made one of his rare mistakes with respect to tutors, and appointed a Bible salesman named Archibald Douglas who proved to be quite normally human, and who introduced Crowley to drinking, smoking, racing, billiards, cards and women. 'The nightmare world of Christianity vanished at the dawn. I fell in with a girl of the theatre in the first ten days at Torquay, and at that touch of human love the detestable mysteries of sex were transformed into joy and beauty. The obsession of sin fell from my shoulders... I found that the world was, after all, full of delightful damned souls. . .' As soon as Uncle Tom found out he got rid of Archibald Douglas, but it was too late.

Crowley's next achievement was to seduce the parlourmaid on his mother's bed. He explains that the girl 'took it into her head to better herself by getting a stranglehold on the young master'. On Sunday morning he made an excuse to stay away from the prayer meeting, 'got the girl into my mother's bedroom and made my magical affirmation'. For some reason, the girl decided to tell on him. Confronted by Uncle Tom, Crowley denied everything, and hit upon an ingenious method of allaying his uncle's suspicions. Pressed to reveal where he had been when the girl alleged they were together, Crowley pretended to be nervous and worried, then finally confessed that he had been buying tobacco. He had already taken the precaution of getting the tobacconist to back up his story. Crowley shed tears and pleaded that he had been led astray by bad companions, and felt doubly triumphant at having got the better of both his uncle and the parlourmaid.

In his book on Crowley, Israel Regardie argues that Crowley had incestuous feelings towards his mother, and that the consummation on her bed proves that he wanted to violate her. This seems to be an unnecessarily Freudian interpretation of Crowley's perfectly straightforward sexual obsession. Sex itself became for him another way of cocking a snook at authority, and if he could combine it with an act of defiance, the pleasure became ten times as great. The key to understanding Crowley is the same as the key to understanding the Marquis de Sade. Both wasted an immense amount of energy screaming defiance at the authority they resented so much, and lacked the insight to see that they were shaking their fists at an abstraction.

The problem with this kind of anti-authoritarianism is that it has the effect of tainting sex with violence and vice versa. The two become associated as gestures of revolt, and it is difficult thereafter to separate them. 'My sexual life was very intense. My relations with women were entirely satisfactory. They gave me the maximum of bodily enjoyment and at the same time symbolized my theological notions of sin. Love was a challenge to Christianity. It was a degradation and a damnation. . .' But he still insists that, sexually speaking, he is perfectly normal, quite free of 'morbid sexual symptoms', which he regards as a symptom of self-division. But, having explained his theory at some length ('The complete man, harmonized, flows freely towards his natural goal'), he then goes on to relate how, at the age of fourteen, he decided to kill a cat to see whether it really had nine lives. 'I therefore caught a cat, and having administered a large dose of arsenic, I chloroformed it, hanged it above the gas jet, stabbed it, cut its throat, smashed its skull and, when it had been pretty thoroughly burnt, drowned it and threw it out of the window that the fall might remove its ninth life. . . I remember that all the time I was genuinely sorry for the animal; I simply forced myself to carry out the experiment in the interest of pure science.' But it is obviously unlikely that even the stupidest fourteen year old could really believe that it is impossible to kill a cat except with nine different forms of violence applied simultaneously; the incident merely illustrates a form of moral imbecility to which Crowley had become prone through sheer hatred of authority.

The anti-authoritarianism developed further when, at the age of sixteen, he was sent to Malvern public school, which he found as 'brutal and imbecile' as the previous one at Cambridge. 'The prefects were hulking louts, shirking both work and play, and concentrating on obscenity and petty tyranny.' And when one of them sought the housemaster's permission to flog Crowley for 'some minor breach of discipline', he found Crowley already there, pouring out his own accusations. 'I got my licking', Crowley reports gleefully, 'but there was a fine series of expulsions to balance it.' Then, aware that what he has just admitted places him in a thoroughly bad light, he hastens to add: 'Of course, my action was technically indefensible; but after all, I had held my tongue uncomplainingly for months and it was only when they appealed to the housemaster to fight their battles that I appealed to him to fight mine.' Crowley is an expert at self-justification; but it takes very little penetration to see through this one—that when he says 'technically indefensible' he means 'morally indefensible', but deliberately chooses the less accurate word, and that when he says 'they' appealed to the housemaster he is trying to gloss over the fact that only one prefect was concerned, and that he chose to inform on them all.

The orgy of tale-telling presumably made him unpopular, and this may have been why he persuaded his mother to take him away from Malvern, which he did with characteristic duplicity. 'I. . . drew such a picture of the abominations which went on, though I knew nothing about them or even what they were, that my mother refused to let me go back. I told her. . . that if Mr Huntingdon [the housemaster] knew what was going on in the house, it would break his heart.' She decided to send him to another public school, Tonbridge, and he records complacently: 'I had developed a kind of natural aristocracy. People were already beginning to be afraid of me.'

Yet here we encounter the essence of the strange paradox that was Aleister Crowley. In page after page of the *Confessions* he emerges as a liar, a sneak, a bully and a hypocrite; we can understand what Regardie meant when he spoke of 'the nasty, petty, vicious louse that occasionally he was on the level of practical human relationships.' Yet a few pages later, dealing with the suggestion that Crowley was a schizophrene (he means a psychopath), Regardie says: 'I do not believe that a schizophrene is capable of the tremendous self-discipline and mental training that Crowley embarked upon.' It would be inaccurate to characterize Crowley as a schizophrene (employing the word in its usual incorrect sense of split-personality) because the split in Crowley was not in the area of the personality. Personality is the aspect of us that copes with the world around us. But the aspect that becomes absorbed in ideas or in work or in beauty is a kind of *im*personality. Impersonality is what Socrates and Michelangelo and Beethoven and Einstein have in common. As a personality, Crowley was inclined to take moral shortcuts; yet another aspect of him could become totally absorbed in work and self-discipline. He loved to be alone, and it is characteristic that his original title for his *Confessions* was *The Spirit of Solitude* (which he borrowed from Shelley). He writes:

> The problem of life was not how to satanise, as Huysmans would have called it; it was simply to escape from oppressors and to enjoy the world without any interference of spiritual life of any sort. My happiest moments were when I was alone on the mountains; but there is no evidence that this pleasure in any way derived from mysticism. The beauty of form and colour, the physical exhilaration of exercise, and the mental stimulation of finding one's way in difficult country, formed the sole elements of my rapture.

[And he adds an interesting piece of self-revelation:]

> So far as I indulged in daydreams, they were exclusively of a normal sexual type. There was no need to create phantasms of a perverse or unrealizable satisfaction. It is important to emphasise this point, because I have always appeared to my contemporaries as a very extraordinary individual obsessed by fantastic passions. But such were not in any way natural to me. The moment the pressure was relieved every touch of the abnormal was shed off instantly. The impulse to write poetry disappeared almost completely at such periods. . .

It is an interesting thought that a Crowley who had been brought up in a non-repressive atmosphere might never have experienced the slightest desire to write poetry, perform ritual magic, or acquire himself the reputation of 'the wickedest man in the world.' On the other hand, he might well have made his mark as an explorer, a scholar or a scientist. As it was, the oversexed schoolboy continued his single-minded pursuit of sin and depravity, and was forced to leave Tonbridge when he caught gonorrhoea from a Glasgow prostitute. His mother felt that he again required the supervision of a Plymouth Brother, and sent him to lodge with one at Eastbourne. He began to attend Eastbourne College and, unexpectedly, discovered an enthusiasm for science. This event—in some ways one of the most important of his life—is dismissed in the *Confessions* in two sentences: 'During the day I worked at Eastbourne College in the chemical laboratory under Professor Hughes, and was privileged to assist the great man in several researches which go to prove that no two substances can combine in the absence of a third. It seems strange that I should have seen the bearings of this upon philosophy.' References to science and mathematics can be found scattered throughout his work, emphasising that they remained lifelong interests. The science writer J.W.N. Sullivan is one of the dedicatees of the *Confessions*, and it is typical that although he seduced Sullivan's wife, Crowley always placed a high value on his friendship.

It was also during the Eastbourne period that Crowley taught himself to play chess and soon discovered that he was the best player in the town. The chess-playing mentality requires the same combination of intuition and logic as the scientist and mathematician; on the other hand, few of the great chess masters have shown remarkable artistic ability. Crowley's powers as a chess player, as well as his natural ability to learn languages, reveal that his cast of mind was objective and scientific rather than artistic. Under different circumstances, he would have made an excellent engineer or city planner.

But the urge to cast off his Christian background had become a neurotic obsession that dominated his life. When his chemistry professor at Eastbourne denounced the Bible, 'it almost took my breath away to hear a man in authority speak so openly.' It never struck Crowley that it might be possible to dismiss Christianity as superstitious nonsense, and then get on with more important things. Crowley's sense of guilt was so strong that defiance of religion had to be a moral crusade. Shaw once remarked of Wagner's obsession with incest that it was all very well, but what sensible person wanted to sleep with his sister? Crowley would have been incapable of this kind of detachment. He records that, on his first stolen visit to the theatre, he looked around at the audience and wondered: 'Aren't all these people afraid of being found out?' So instead of trying to make use of his natural talent for science or languages, he continued to look around for a career that would 'shock the bourgeoisie' and outrage their moral standards.

Writing poetry seemed a step in the right direction. At Malvern he had written a poem in honour of Florence Maybrick, sentenced to death (later commuted to life imprisonment) for poisoning her husband, who objected to her affair with a certain Mr Brierly.

> Poor lady! whom a wicked jury's hate
> In face of facts as iron as the grave
> To which they would have doomed thee – bitter fate!
> Thee guiltless to the cruel hangman gave.

Crowley admitted that his sympathy for Mrs Maybrick 'nowise argues my belief in her innocence. She was admittedly an adulteress. I asked no further questions. The mere fact thrilled me to the marrow. Adultery being the summit of wickedness, its commision excused everything.'

The earliest influence on Crowley's poetry was Swinburne:

> Are the roses dead to-day?
> Is the wine spilt? Is the flute
> Broken? Is thy lover fled?
> Has the dancer danced away?
> Is the voice of ocean mute?
> Is the hour of dreamland dead?
> Nay, the slumbers of thine head
> Shall be until thy lures,
> Love shall gird thee as a garment
> while thy very life endures.

But it can be seen that he lacks Swinburne's natural talent for verbal music; his poetry never seems to flow freely for more than a line or two. Then he seems to get himself tangled up in language:

> Ere the grape of joy is golden
> With the summer and the sun
> Ere the maidens unbeholden
> Gather one by one,
> To the vineyard comes the shower,
> No sweet rain to fresh the flower,
> But the thunder rain that cleaves,
> Rends and ruins tender leaves.

'Fresh the flower' sounds awkward, and the last three lines have to be read several times to grasp their meaning.

Even in the nature poetry, where there is a more obvious sincerity, there is this same odd clumsiness:

> Blind the iron pinnacles edge the twilight;
> Blind and black the gills of the mountain clefted,

Crag and snow-clad slope in a distant vision
Rise as before me.

At the age of twenty, Crowley was trying to build a career
on a complete misconception of his natural talents. This was,
in fact, the year he went up to Cambridge. The Eastbourne
period had ended in an unusually violent eruption. He lived
with his tutor's family, and sympathised strongly with the
middle daughter, a 'beautiful, voluptuous and normal' girl
who was engaged to an equally normal young man. But the
family insisted that they could only marry on condition he
became a Plymouth Brother. When the young man decided
against it, he was thrown out of the house, and the girl was
subjected to continuous abuse and ill-treatment. 'Meals were
a poisoned whirlwind. . .' 'One morning at breakfast I said
about a millionth part of what I thought and the family started
screaming. It was as if they had been attacked by a collective
mania. Everything was thrown at me; they went for me with
claws and fists. They were too blind with rage to know what
they were doing. I simply knocked their heads together and
walked out of the house. When I thought the atmosphere had
had time to dissipate I returned with the intention of carrying
out a rescue for the distressed damsel. They were too much
scared to oppose me, and I begged her to come away at once
and go to her ex-fiancé's family. But she could not summon
up courage to do it. . . later in the afternoon my Uncle Tom,
summoned by telegram, came to fetch me away from the
accursed spot. . .'
    Crowley's language, as on so many other occasions,
obscures what actually happened. Did they physically attack
him? Did he physically attack them? At all events, it seems to
have confirmed Crowley's feeling that people were afraid of
him. 'The incident had a wholesome effect upon my own
family. They had failed to break my spirit and begun to realize
that I had reached the stage when I could make as much
trouble for them as they could for me. The best thing they
could do was to let me go my own way. I had won the fight;
and the evidence was my season in the Bernese Oberland on
my own responsibility. I was recalled by telegram. They had
decided to let me go to Trinity.'
    It was the beginning of a new epoch in his life. 'I had the

sensation of drawing a long deep breath as one does after swimming under water. . .' He was intoxicated with freedom, and took advantage of it to read all kinds of books he had never been allowed to read—Carlyle, Swift, Coleridge, Fielding, Gibbon—and to have as many sexual liaisons as possible. '. . . at Cambridge I discovered that I was of an intensely passionate nature, physiologically speaking. My poetic instincts, further, transformed the most sordid liaisons into romance, so that the impossibility of contracting a suitable and serious relation did not worry me.' There was no prostitution in Cambridge, 'but nearly all the younger women of the district are eager to co-operate in the proper spirit.' Even so, he found the time he had to devote to pursuing them a continual irritation. He records in the autobiography that he resents the system that makes it necessary to waste so much time pursuing something that ought to be delivered with the milk. And while Crowley found women necessary to satisfy his physical needs, he found them unsatisfying as human beings. 'Intellectually. . . they did not exist. Even the few whose minds were not completely blank had them furnished with Wardour Street Chippendale. Their attainments were those of the ape and the parrot. These facts did not deter me. On the contrary, it was highly convenient that one's sexual relations should be with an animal. . .' Crowley was devoid of the element of protectiveness on which most successful male-female partnerships are based, so it is unsurprising that most of his long-term sexual relationships ended in disaster.

He decided to enter the diplomatic service because 'it seemed to afford the greatest opportunities for worldly enjoyment.' The court that appealed to him most was that of Imperial Russia, and he went to St Petersburg in the long vacation of 1897. It was on his way back from Russia that he attended a chess congress in Berlin, and suddenly decided that he no longer wanted to be world champion. Watching these shabby nonentities 'I perceived with preternatural lucidity that I had not alighted on this planet with the object of playing chess.'

But what *had* he alighted on it for? On the last day of the previous year, he had had a strange mystical experience in Stockholm that seemd to give him a glimpse of his way forward:

I was awakened to the knowledge that I possessed a magical means of becoming conscious of and satisfying a part of my nature which had up to that moment concealed itself from me. It was an experience of horror and pain, combined with a certain ghostly terror, yet at the same time it was the key to the purest and holiest spiritual ecstasy that exists. At the time, I was not aware of the supreme importance of the matter. It seemed to me little more than a development of certain magical processes with which I was already familiar. . .

It is obvious that Crowley is quite determined to speak in riddles. In *The Great Beast*, Symonds suggests that 'he had an illumination that he could control reality by magical thinking.' If so, why did he not say so? When Crowley is reticent in the *Confessions*, it is usually on account of the censor (for example, he fails to mention that he left Tonbridge school because he caught gonorrhoea). Moreover, the comment that it seemed to be a 'development of certain magical processes already known to me' also seems to afford a clue, for in 1896, when he was only twenty-one, Crowley still knew nothing about magic—that only came about two years later, when he met an alchemist called Julian Baker. The only 'magic' he refers to in the *Confessions* before that date is sex magic, as, for example, when he says that he made his 'magical affirmation' with the parlour maid on his mother's bed. We should also take note of the words 'I possessed a magical means of becoming conscious of and satisfying *a part of my nature* which had up to that moment concealed itself from me.' What part of his nature had so far concealed itself from him? The obvious answer is surely: his homosexuality. So far, Crowley's sexuality had been, as he never tires of emphasising, completely normal— so that he remarks about his early period at Cambridge: 'My skill in avoiding corporal punishment and my lack of opportunity for inflicting it had saved me from developing the sadistic or masochistic sides to my character.' It there- fore seems probable that the revelation that came to Crowley in Stockholm was of his homosexual tendencies, or per- haps his inherent masochism and the possibility of satis- fying it by becoming the passive partner in acts of sodomy.

Symonds' mistake probably arises from the fact that Crowley says that the revelation took place at midnight on 31

December 1896, and that he was 'awakened' to the magical knowledge; it sounds as if Crowley woke up from sleep. But 31 December is New Year's Eve, and it is more likely that Crowley was enjoying the New Year's Eve celebrations when some homosexual encounter made him aware of this element in his own nature.

This matter is connected with another curious minor mystery about Crowley's development. 1895, the year he went up to Cambridge, was also the year of the trial of Oscar Wilde. Wilde and Crowley had a great deal in common; in fact, Wilde's attitude to sin and to Christian morality is so close to Crowley's own that Crowley often sounds as if he is echoing Wilde. We know that Crowley was swept off his feet by the poetry of Swinburne; it seems unbelievable that he was not equally enraptured by Wilde's *Sphinx* and *Picture of Dorian Grey*. Yet the only lengthy passage about Wilde in the *Confessions* takes a patronising tone, and implies that Wilde became a homosexual simply as a method of getting to know 'the right people' at Oxford. This negative attitude towards a man Crowley might have been expected to admire wholeheartedly arouses the inevitable suspicion that Crowley was influenced by Wilde, but for some reason preferred not to acknowledge it. The last thing he wanted was to be labelled a kind of imitation-Oscar. And this, in turn, gives rise to another suspicion: that Crowley's homosexual experiment may have been inspired by Wilde, and by a certain romanticism about the 'love that dare not speak its name.' This, at all events, is a suspicion that seems consistent with the facts.

In 1897, the year he went to Russia, Crowley experienced another 'dark night of the soul' that was to profoundly affect his whole mental outlook. It was during an illness, a few months after his return from St Petersburg, that he went through a period of deep depression, during which he found himself 'forced to meditate upon the fact of mortality.' 'I was appalled by the futility of all human endeavour.' Suddenly, all life seemed pointless. What if he became England's ambassador to Paris? His name would be forgotten in a hundred years. What if he became a great poet? He was in one of England's two great universities, yet hardly anyone knew anything about Aeschylus. Suppose he became a Homer or Shakespeare, a Caesar or Napoleon: what would it all matter when the earth finally disappeared?

Instead of concluding that this gloomy view was simply the outcome of illness and too many hangovers, Crowley allowed himself to be convinced that he was contemplating some profound universal truth—in fact, the first of the Buddha's four noble truths: the recognition that life is nothing but suffering. This led him to decide: 'I must find a material in which to work which is immune from the forces of change.' 'Brain and body were valueless except as instruments of the soul'. 'The ordinary materialist usually fails to recognize that only spiritual affairs count for anything, even in the grossest concerns of life. . . Material welfare is only important as assisting men towards a consciousness of satisfaction.' This is obviously a profoundly important recognition, and reveals that, for all his faults, Crowley was capable of thinking his way through to important insights. The businessman strives for wealth as if wealth in itself could provide a means of satisfaction; other men strive for fame, for power, for sexual conquest, for the same reason. But most of these things turn out to be curiously disappointing. This is because our real aim is to achieve power over *the mind itself*, and without this power, all 'achievement' is futile.

But having achieved this important insight, which sounds like the beginning of wisdom, Crowley proceeded to subject it to his own peculiarly twisted logic. 'From the nature of things, therefore, life is a sacrament; in other words, all our acts are magical acts. Our spiritual consciousness acts through the will and its instruments upon material objects, in order to produce changes which will result in the establishment of the new conditions of consciousness which we wish. That is the definition of Magick.' (Crowley preferred to spell it with a 'k' to distinguish it from the common use of 'magic'.) He then goes on to admit:

But I was so far from perceiving that every act is magical, whether one likes it or not, that I supposed the escape from matter to involve a definite invasion of the spiritual world. Indeed, I was so far from understanding that matter was in its nature secondary and symbolic, that my principal preoccupation was to obtain first-hand sensory evidence of spiritual beings.

In other words, I wanted to evoke the denizens of other planes to visible and audible appearance.

But *which* denizens? For Crowley, there were two sides: angels and devils:

> On the Christian hypothesis the reality of evil makes the devil equal to God. [And if I had to take sides, then] it was not difficult to make up my mind. The forces of good were those which had constantly oppressed me. I saw them daily destroying the happiness of my fellow men. Since, therefore it was my business to experience the spiritual world, my first step must be to get into personal communication with the devil.

In order to understand this Alice in Wonderland logic, which will strike most people as unintentionally funny, we have to grasp that Crowley had suffered so much from religious idiots that the very word 'goodness' aroused a Pavlovian reaction of fury. He possessed a powerful, logical mind; it should have been easy enough to see that real goodness is another name for human decency, and has nothing to do with religious bigotry. But while his mother and Uncle Tom were, figuratively speaking, breathing down his neck, he was unable to exercise normal logic. So, like some latter-day Faust, Crowley decided that the correct response to his Vision of Universal Suffering was to try and raise demons. He went to the nearest bookseller and asked for a work on ritual magic. He was handed a compilation called *The Book of Black Magic and Pacts* by A. E. Waite, a member of the Golden Dawn. Crowley found this thoroughly disappointing; it seemed to be full of spells for preventing a huntsman from killing game or bewitching a neighbour's cows. This was not the real stuff of diabolism, as revealed in Huysmans' novel *Là-Bas*, with its Black Masses and sexual orgies. But a passage in the book seemed to hint that Waite knew of some Hidden Church which preserved the mysteries of true initiation. Crowley wrote to Waite, who replied with a letter advising him to read a book called *The Cloud upon the Sanctuary* by Karl von Eckartshausen, an eighteenth century German mystic who wrote about precisely such a secret religious order.

Crowley read it again and again, and became obsessed by the idea of reaching this secret order:

> The sublimity of the idea enthralled me; it satisfied my craving for romance and poetry. I determined with my whole heart to make myself worthy to attract the notice of this mysterious brotherhood. I yearned passionately for illumination. I could imagine nothing more exquisite than to enter into communion with these holy men and to acquire the power of communicating with the angelic and divine intelligence of the universe.

All this was at least a little more satisfying than the Celtic Church, a curious communion of which he had become a member, and which 'moved in an atmosphere of fairies, seal women and magical operations'. The Celtic Church had made Crowley dream of going in quest of the Holy Grail; while membership of another movement, the Spanish Legitimists (which wished to place Don Carlos on the throne of Spain) led him to dream of becoming a man of action; but Don Carlos changed his mind and the conspiracy collapsed. Crowley was in a state of spiritual flux, possessed by contradictory yearnings to become a member of a secret order of saints and a devil worshipper.

Mountain climbing continued to obsess him; he was an excellent climber, who had taught himself by scrambling up Cumberland fells and Beachy Head, then began to spend every holiday in the Alps or Bernese Oberland. He found an opportunity to express some of his innate inclination to hero worship when he met an experienced mountaineer called Oscar Eckenstein in the Lake District. Eckenstein was a scientist, and he set out to teach Crowley all about the techniques of climbing; it seems clear that he became the father figure Crowley had seen searching for ever since the death of his father.

A completely different kind of friendship sprang up between Crowley and a female impersonator named Herbert Pollitt, ten years Crowley's senior, who came to Cambridge to take part in the Footlights revue. Pollitt had long, pale-gold hair, and tragic eyes, and 'his outlook on life was desperate.' Crowley admits that 'the relation between us was that ideal intimacy which the Greeks considered the greatest glory of manhood', but then deliberately sets out to mislead when he adds that the English connect such ideas with physical passion. There can be little doubt that the relationship with Pollitt was Crowley's first fully-fledged homosexual affair. Pollitt was a friend of Aubrey Beardsley, and introduced Crowley to the work of other 'decadent' writers and artists. (This is why it seems incomprehensible that Crowley makes no mention of having read Wilde.) 'In his heart was a hunger for beauty which I can only call hideous and cruel, because it was so hopeless.' But Pollitt felt that Crowley's 'spiritual aspirations'—the yearning to join some secret brotherhood—were futile and pointless, and Crowley finally decided to break with him. In spite of his own tendency to pessimism, there was an instinct for health in Crowley that led him to turn his back on the feeble and the defeated.

Nevertheless, the twenty-two-year-old Crowley was a thoroughly mixed-up young man, a poor little rich boy, a snob who was not quite certain of his own social position, an incorrigible exhibitionist who was unsure of his own identity, a bully with a craving to be loved, a diabolist with a paradoxical desire to be a saint. The autobiography, written in his fifties, still reveals a festering ego, brooding on the humiliations of more than thirty years ago, and descending to a silly kind of abuse that suggests that his mental age is still that of an adolescent:

[A.E. Waite] is not only the most ponderously platitudinous and priggishly prosaic of pretentiously pompous pork butchers of the language, but the most voluminously voluble. I cannot dig over the dreary deserts of his drivel in search of the passage which made me write to him. . .

He devotes a full page to reviling the English Alpine Club, insisting that it was 'bitterly opposed to mountaineering—its members were incompetent, insanely jealous of their vested interest and unthinkably unsportsmanlike.' The reason for this abuse, it emerges, is that the Club had turned down his own admission for membership. Why? Because 'the record of climbs I put in for admission was much too good.' And we have to read between the lines, and call upon our knowledge of Crowley's character, to realise that they must have found him intolerably cocky and boastful. If Crowley had been alive half a century earlier, we might suspect that he was the model for Flashman in *Tom Brown's Schooldays*.

But the boastful exhibitionist also had a genuine desire to find some cause to which he could devote his life. Literature seemed to be the obvious choice—since his poetry flowed freely and naturally—but even here he could not make up his mind where the poet ended and the poseur began. John Symonds began the original edition of *The Great Beast* with this quotation from Crowley's first published poem *Aceldama*, which is an apt illustration of the problem:

It was a windy night, that memorable seventh night of December, when this philosophy was born in me. How the grave old professor wondered at my ravings! I had called at his house, for he was a valued friend of mine, and I felt strange thoughts and emotions shake within me. Ah! how I raved! I called on him to trample me, he would not. We passed together into the stormy night. I was on horseback, how I galloped round him in my phrensy, till he became the prey of real physical fear! How I shrieked out I know not what strange words! And the poor good old man tried all he could to calm me; he thought I was mad! The fool! I was in the death struggle with self; God and Satan fought for my soul those three long hours. God conquered—now I have only one doubt left— which of the twain was God?

Even the title of the poem (Aceldama was the field bought with Judas's thirty pieces of silver) brings to mind W.S. Gilbert's parody of Swinburne from *Patience*:

> Oh! to be wafted away
> From this black Aceldama of sorrow,
> Where the earth of a dusty today
> Is the dust of an earthy tomorrow!

In the *Confessions* Crowley writes: 'But in *Aceldama*. . . I attained, at a bound, the summit of Parnassus. In a sense, I have never written anything better.' But when, in 1910, he issued a selection of his poems 'in response to a widely-spread lack of interest in my writings. . .' he took care not to include anything from *Aceldama*. It is, in fact, a typical Crowleyan rhapsody to sin, whoredom and degradation.

Aceldama was the first of a series of poems and dramas that he printed at his own expense; in 1898 alone he published, in addition to *Aceldama: The Tale of Archais, Songs of the Spirit, The Poem, Jephthah, Jezebel* and *White Stains*. The last is a collection

of obscene poems which professes to be the literary remains
of a 'neuropath of the Second Empire.' In the *Confessions* he
claims, typically, that the book proves his 'essential spirituality..
and preternatural innocence.' He explains that he had been
reading Krafft-Ebing's *Psychopathia Sexualis*, and disagreed
that sexual perversions are the result of disease. They are,
ays Crowley, 'merely magical affirmations of perfectly intel-
ligible points of view'. Crowley thought that since his pervert
ended in madness and murder, he had written a highly moral
book that was suitable for Sunday schools.

But poetry can be an unsatisfactory means of expression,
particularly when no one buys it or reads it. Crowley was still
obsessed with thoughts of magic. At Wastdale Head, he had
'appealed with the whole force of my will to the adepts of the
Hidden Church to prepare me as a postulant for that august
company. As will be seen later, acts of will, performed by the
proper person, never fall to the ground. . .' This seemed to
have no immediate effect. But he continued to read 'occult'
texts in a desultory kind of way, struggling through Knorr von
Rosenroth's *Kabbalah Unveiled*, translated by S.L. MacGregor
Mathers, and through various works on alchemy. In Zermatt
in 1898, he found himself among a group of Englishmen in a
beer hall, and began to 'lay down the law on alchemy.' 'I trust I
impressed the group of men with my vast learning.' But one
of the party proved to be a real alchemist—a chemist named
Julian L. Baker. He walked back with Crowley to his hotel, and
revealed that he himself had succeeded in 'fixing' mercury—
turning the liquid into a solid. Crowley was immediately
convinced that this was the Master for whom he had sent out
his SOS signal the previous Easter at Wastdale. But the next
day, Baker had left the hotel. Frantically, Crowley telegraphed
all over the valley, and finally caught up with Baker ten miles
below Zermatt. 'I told him of my search for the Secret
Sanctuary of the Saints and convinced him of my desperate
earnestness. He hinted that he knew of an Assembly which
might be that for which I was looking.'

Back in London, Baker met Crowley, and introduced him
to a man whom he described as 'much more of a Magician
than I am.' This man proved to be George Cecil Jones, an
analytical chemist who looked like Jesus Christ, and who had
a fiery and unstable temper. It was Jones who finally told

Crowley about the Hermetic Order of the Golden Dawn, founded ten years earlier, and introduced him to MacGregor Mathers. Crowley paid his ten shillings membership fee, and on November 18, 1898, attended the Mark Masons' Hall in Great Queen Street and was given the magical name *Perdurabo* (I will endure), then he went through the solemn, if rather absurd, magical ceremony that made him a member of the Golden Dawn. His SOS had been answered.

Three
Raising Hell

THE CHIEF of the Golden Dawn, Samuel Liddell Mathers, was quite as extraordinary a character as Crowley himself. The poet Yeats, who met Mathers in the British Museum Reading Room around the beginning of the 1890s, noticed:

> . . . a man of thirty-six or thirty-seven, in a brown velveteen coat, with a gaunt resolute face and an athletic body, who seemed. . . to be a figure of romance. . . I believe that his mind in those early days did not belie his face and body—though in later years it became unhinged as Don Quixote's was unhinged—for he kept a proud head amid great poverty. One that boxed with him nightly has told me that for many weeks he could knock him down, though Mathers was the stronger man, and only knew long after that during those weeks Mathers starved.

It would be possible for a hostile biographer to see Mathers as almost a figure of fun. Born in Hackney, East London, in 1854, Mathers was the son of a clerk, and became a clerk himself when he left school. He joined the Hampshire Infantry Volunteers in his twenties, and there is a photograph of him in lieutenant's uniform. But he does not figure in the regiment's list of officers, so we must assume that he was a private or, at most, an NCO. The officer's rank seems to be a sign of his extremely active fantasy life, like the titles 'MacGregor of Glenstrae' and 'Count of Glenstrae' that he later awarded himself. At the age of twenty-three he became a Mason; it was through the Masons that he met the London coroner Dr Wynn Westcott, and Dr William Woodman, who introduced him to the English branch of the Rosicrucians. Mathers became their protegé, and they commissioned him to translate *The Kabbalah Unveiled*. Then the famous 'cypher manuscripts' turned up—according to the most popular

version, on a second-hand bookstall in the Farringdon
Road—and the Golden Dawn was founded. In the previous
year, 1887, Mathers had met a beautiful French art student in
the British Museum, Moina Bergson, sister of the philosopher,
and eventually persuaded her to marry him and share his
poverty. She had strong psychic gifts, and Mathers used her
as a 'seeress'. By now, Mathers was calling himself 'MacGregor'
and allowing it to be understood that he was the chief of the
clan. He liked to be photographed in highland regalia.

It sounds then, as if he was an incorrigible fantasist, a
dreamer who found the dull reality of his life as Samuel
Mathers, underpaid clerk, impossible to bear, and who
promoted himself to the rank which he felt to be more in
accord with his nobility of spirit. But this would undoubtedly
be a mistake. Whatever his pretensions, his 'magical powers'
were real enough. Mathers handed Yeats various 'tattwa
symbols' (yellow squares, blue discs, red triangles, etc), and
when Yeats pressed them against his forehead, he began to
see images that he could not control: a desert, with a black
giant rising up among ancient ruins. Mathers told him he had
seen a being of the order of the salamanders—fire elementals—
because he had used the fire symbol. Yeats was at first
inclined to think that these odd tricks were the result of
imagination or telepathy, until constant experience convinced
him that the symbols actually conjured up the appropriate
image, and that when he accidentally gave someone the
wrong symbol, it still conjured up the correct image. The
same symbol—a star—evoked in one subject a vision of a
rough stone house with the skull of a horse in it, and in
another, a rough stone house with a golden skeleton it it. The
similarity was too great to be accidental. At another session
with Mathers and his wife, all three participated in lengthy
hallucinations, Yeats seeing in brief flashes what Mrs Mathers
was describing, and often seeing things before she described
them. Even if these visions were merely form of imagination,
it still seems obvious that some peculiar power was at work.
So whether or not we can accept that these phenomena were
'magical' or merely psychological, there can be no doubt that
Mathers had stumbled on some interesting secrets, and that
he was not a fraud in the ordinary sense of the word.

What seems altogether more dubious is his apparently

sincere belief that he was in touch with 'Secret Masters.' In 1892, Mathers became convinced that he had contacted these Masters, and that this confirmed his position as head of the Golden Dawn. In a manifesto issued four years later, Mathers declared that the Secret Chiefs were human and living on earth, but possessed of terrible superhuman powers. He claimed that contact with these chiefs was a frightening experience:

> I can only compare it to the continued effect of that usually experienced momentarily by any person close to whom a flash of lightning passes during a violent storm; coupled with a difficulty in respiration similar to the half-strangling effect produced by ether.

We are naturally inclined to dismiss this kind of thing as pure imagination, that is, a deliberate lie. But before doing so, it is important to bear in mind that this 'occult tradition' of secret masters is not a modern invention, dating from Madame Blavatsky. It *is* genuinely a part of an ancient tradition, and it can be found in many religions of the world. The composer Cyril Scott expressed its essence when he wrote in *An Outline of Modern Occultism* (1935):

> Firstly, the occultist holds that Man is in process of evolving from comparative imperfection to much higher states of physical and spiritual evolution. Secondly, that the evolutionary process in all its phases is directed by a Great Hierarchy of Intelligences who have themselves reached these higher states.

One of the best modern expositions of this notion is to be found in *The People of the Secret* by Edward Campbell (writing under the pseudonym Ernest Scott), who starts from the notion of a 'Hidden Directorate', referred to in Sufic tradition; Campbell identifies this directorate with a concept to be found in *The Dramatic Universe* by J.G. Bennett, a follower of Gurdjieff: of 'a class of cosmic essences called Demiurges that is responsible for maintaining the universal order.' *The People of the Secret* is an interpretation of western history in terms of this notion: of deliberate intervention in human history by these 'Demiurgic Intelligences'. He sees the concept of these Intelligences as part of an occult tradition that can be traced from the Sufis, which entered Europe through the Arab invasion of Spain, and which also finds expression in the Tarot, the Kabbalah and alchemy.

It should be mentioned at this point that the Hebrew 'magical' system known as the Kabbalah is the foundation stone of western occultism. Its basic notion is that there are ten levels of reality, of which the one on which we live—the earthly plane—is the lowest. A kind of magical tree, the tree of life, connects these planes, rather like the beanstalk in the fairy tale. But they must also be seen as inner worlds, or planes of consciousness, which man can explore if he has enough mental discipline.

This 'exploration' has much in common with a technique devised by Carl Jung, which he called 'active imagination.' At a period of mental crisis before the First World War, Jung discovered that he could enter into states which might be described as waking dreams, and in these states, he held conversations with beings he was convinced were real, that is, who existed independently of his own mind. Jung's belief that there are realms of the mind that are common to us all—like some inner country—is closely related to the ideas of the Kabbalists. It may also be significant that Jung came to feel that alchemical texts offer a kind of symbolic guide to these inner realms.

It is possible to see then, that although Mathers sounds like a self-deceiving crank, he was actually working within a well-established tradition, and was convinced that he had simply been fortunate enough (with the help of the Secret Chiefs) to gain access to an ancient knowledge system virtually forgotten by western man. He believed that he had been influenced and guided by the Chiefs from an early point in his life.

So we may regard Mathers as an extremely fascinating psychological case, a romantic dreamer who wove around himself an extraordinarily complete web of self-delusion. Or we may regard him as a remarkable 'outsider', like so many of the great poets and artists of the nineteenth century, who chose to walk his own lonely path, sustained by a certainty that came from 'inner vision.' This is the way that Crowley saw him when he met him in 1898. At the time of the meeting, Mathers had been living in Paris for the past six years. He was partly supported by another Golden Dawn member, Annie

Horniman—the tea heiress—but eventually quarrelled with her, and suspended her membership. So life in Paris was as poverty-stricken as in London. And it was hard to maintain his authority as head of the Golden Dawn from Paris. (Mathers was the sort of person to whom maintaining his authority was of major importance.) So when Crowley, with his capacity for hero-worship and his craving for father-figures, presented himself in Paris, Mathers immediately accepted him as a friend and ally. They had much in common: both were egoists; both were proud and dictatorial; both were inclined to make a fetish of physical fitness and athleticism; both were snobs, and liked to fantasize about belonging to the aristocracy. When Crowley turned on his Libran charm, he was hard to resist. Mathers was completely won over.

Other members of the Golden Dawn were less enthusiastic. To the romantic Yeats, Crowley must have seemed insufferably bouncy and conceited. Crowley thought Yeat's work 'lacked virility.' When he called on Yeats, he took with him the proofs of his play *Jephthah*, of which the following is a typical extract:

Oh the time of dule and teen!
Oh the dove the hawk has snared!
Would to God we had not been,
We, who see our maiden queen,
Love has slain whom hate has spared.

Yeats probably thought it was derivative rubbish, but was too polite to say so. 'He forced himself to utter a few polite conventionalities.' But Crowley felt he could see through to the 'black, bilious rage that shook him to the soul', because he instantly recognized Crowley's incomparable superiority as a poet. Crowley adds charitably that he saw this as proof that Yeats was a genuine poet, because no charlatan would have felt such fear of a greater poet than himself. . .

Meanwhile, Crowley had taken himself a flat in Chancery Lane, and dedicated a mirror-lined room as a temple for white magic. There was also a black temple, whose altar was supported by a statue of a negro standing on his hands. It also contained a skeleton, which Crowley 'fed' with blood, and to which he sacrificed small birds—the idea being to give it life. Crowley shared the flat with another Golden Dawn member named Alan Bennett, one of the few members who took a liking to him. Bennett seems to have been a man of extremely strong personality, and he introduced himself to Crowley by looking into his eyes and saying in almost menacing tones: 'Little brother, you have been meddling with the Goetia' (black magic). When Crowley denied it, Bennett said: 'Then the Goetia has been meddling with you.' In fact, Crowley was convinced that Yeats was trying to put a spell on him, out of jealousy of his poetry, so he was much impressed. As he got to know Bennett better, he must also have been impressed by his way of life. Bennett suffered from asthma, to alleviate which he took opium; then, after a month, he would find himself becoming accustomed to it, and instead of increasing the dose, would switch to morphine, then to cocaine, then to chloroform. When he was weak enough, the asthma would go away, and return as he became stronger. He seems to have had a Swiftian loathing for human physical functions, including sex and childbirth. Crowley became deeply attached to him.

By now, Crowley was calling himself Count Vladimir Svareff, and no doubt speaking with an appropriate Russian accent. He explains in the *Confessions* that it was a psychological experiment, to see how people would treat a Russian nobleman. In fact, he was probably influenced by Mathers—'MacGregor of Glenstrae'—and by his own incorrigible egoism.

But the desire to be a magician was undoubtedly genuine. In his Chancery Lane temple, he was practising the magic of Abra-Melin the Mage, a forgotten magician Mathers had discovered in the Bibliothèque Nationale in Paris, and translated into English. Abra-Melin's rituals differ markedly from those of other grimoires, for example, the *Key of Solomon* or *Sword of Moses*, with their solemn invocation of demons— all performed from within a magic circle; by comparison, Abra-Melin is quiet and almost mystical in tone, and the invocations sound like prayers. No magic circle or pentacle is required—merely a 'holy place, such as an altar constructed in a wood. For six months, the magician must 'inflame himself with prayer'. If he is successful, his Holy Guardian Angel will manifest himself, and he will instruct the magician in good and evil spirits.

Crowley began practising Abra-Melin magic in his Chancery Lane temple, with the help of Bennett and his friend Jones.

And he seems to have obtained almost immediate results. There is no need to disbelieve him when he says 'during this time, magical phenomena were of constant occurrence', although we may suspect that all Crowley was doing was to involve himself in some form of 'spiritualism' not unlike table-turning or playing with an Ouija board. Anyone who sits around in the dark, trying to invoke spirits for long enough, will probably obtain some unusual results. The classic experiment—performed many years after Crowley's death—was devised by the Toronto Society for Psychical Research, who decided to 'conjure up' a spirit they had invented themselves, an English nobleman called Philip who had committed suicide after his mistress was burned as a witch. After a while, raps sounded from a table, and the entity identified itself—by means of a code—as Philip, and told his life story in some detail. Later on, the 'possessed' table appeared on television and walked up on to the platform by rocking back and forth up the steps. The Toronto group was convinced that they had proved that 'spirits' are the creation of the unconscious mind; but an equally plausible hypothesis is that they succeeded in invoking the kind of dubious entity that often manifests at seances.[1]

At all events, Crowley found that 'demons' came unsought, and that semi-solid shadows were appearing on the stairs. He locked the temple door before leaving for dinner with Jones; when he came back, it was open, and the furniture had been disarranged and symbols flung on the floor—typical poltergeist activity.

Crowley and Jones decided that Bennett would die unless he could be sent to a warmer climate. The problem was that Bennett was Crowley's teacher, and Crowley felt strongly that it is a violation of the laws of magic to accept money. He and Jones invoked the spirit Buer, the healer of the sick, and he claims that they saw a helmeted head and a solid left leg, although the rest was cloudy. The operation had to be accounted a failure.

Then Crowley had an idea. He was having a love affair with the wife of a colonel—Crowley rejected the idea that the

1. See *Conjuring up Philip, An Adventure in Psychokinesis* by Iris M. Owen and Margaret Sparrow. FitzHenry and Whiteside, Toronto.

aspiring magician must be strictly chaste—and had been trying to get rid of her. The woman begged Crowley to see her at her hotel. Crowley went, and told her he would offer her the opportunity of doing a completely unselfish act—to give him a hundred pounds for a friend. She handed over the money, and Bennett was able to sail for Ceylon, where he became a Buddhist monk. John Symonds makes the not implausible suggestion that the real reason Crowley decided not to give Bennett the money himself was that he was less rich than he pretended to be, and was running through his inheritance at an alarming speed.

It was obvious that London was no place to carry out the full ritual prescribed by Abra-Melin the Mage—to begin with, it takes six months to complete. Crowley required a house with a door opening to the north, outside which there had to be a terrace that he could cover with fine river sand, and a 'lodge' where the spirits could congregate. He searched throughout most of 1899, and finally found what he wanted on the southern shore of Loch Ness, near Foyers—it was called Boleskine House, and its owner was willing to rent it. Crowley decided to follow Mathers' practice and award himself a title: he called himself the Laird of Boleskine and Abertarff, and purchased the appropriate tartan. Then Frater Perdurabo—the magical name given him by the Golden Dawn—began preparing the talismans he would need for the Abra-Melin ritual. The immediate result was a strange shadow that made it necessary to use artificial light, even on the brightest day. After that, the house 'became peopled with shadowy shapes', and a friend who had come to stay with him was suddenly seized with panic, and left without saying goodbye. Then, as mentioned earlier in this book, his coachman became an alcoholic, his housekeeper vanished, and a workman went mad and tried to kill Crowley. Still the Laird persisted with his invocations, and practised kabbalistic techniques of astral travel, seeing visions of fire angels, earth spirits and other elementals.

But Crowley was not the kind of person to persist in fasting, prayer and meditation for six months—not to mention abstinence from sex. He became bored with trying to 'uplift the standard of Sacrifice and Sorrow', and began to brood vengefully on his fellow magicians of the Golden Dawn. They were definitely hostile. Mathers had initiated Crowley into a higher grade in Paris, and they felt it should have been done in consultation with the London Lodge. So when Crowley applied for the documents to which he believed he was entitled, he was refused. Julian Baker admitted that he thought Mathers was behaving badly. The actress Florence Farr, who was nominally in charge of the London group, felt that she could no longer be Mather's representative and sent him a letter offering her resignation. Mathers scented defiance, and sent her an angry letter in the course of which he denounced Wynn Westcott, the original founder of the Golden Dawn, and accused him of forging the original 'Sprengel' documents. This meant that, in effect, the London Lodge was based on a lie. But this did not apply to the Paris Lodge, for Mathers himself had been in contact with the Secret Chiefs since 1892, and had founded a 'Second Order' under their direction. All this aroused rage and consternation in London.

Crowley immediately wrote to Mathers, offering his full support, and his fortune as well. Then he rushed off to Paris, where he had no difficulty persuading Mathers to appoint him his representative in dealing with the London Lodge. Crowley had no doubt that Mathers had every right to be as high-handed as he pleased. He writes typically: 'My own attitude was unhampered by any ethical considerations. . . Ordinary morality is only for ordinary people.' The London 'rebels' deserved to be squashed like beetles. (Crowley also seems to have taken the colonel's wife with him on this trip to Paris, as a reward for giving Bennett the £100.) Then he hurried back to London, chortling at the idea of getting his own back on the people who had snubbed him. His chief task was to interrogate all the 'rebels' and force them to sign a pledge of loyalty to Mathers. His immediate purpose was to seize the temple—or vault—in which members were initiated into the Second Order (it was supposed to be a replica of the vault in which the body of the legendary Christian Rosenkreuz, founder of the Rosicrucians, had been found in 1604). Crowley engaged a chucker-out from a pub in Leicester Square, then went, together with his latest mistress, Elaine Simpson, to the rooms in Blythe Road, Hammersmith. The lady who was there sent a frantic telegram to another Golden

Dawn member named Hunter; he and Florence Farr arrived
to find Crowley asserting that he was now in possession of the
vault. A constable was sent for, who persuaded Crowley to
leave. The next day, he was back wearing Highland dress,
with a black mask over his face and a dagger at his side. This
time, Yeats was there with Hunter, and refused Crowley
admittance. Again a policeman was sent for, and again
Crowley and his mistress were ordered to leave. The chucker-
out finally arrived—having got lost en route—too late to
support Crowley. In a letter to Lady Gregory, Yeats explained
that they had been forced to throw Mathers out of the Order,
after he had sent one 'Crowley, a quite unspeakable person', to
try to seize the headquarters. He explained that they had re-
fured to admit Crowley into the Second Order 'because we did
not think a mystical society was intended to be a reformatory.'

Next Crowley tried the law, but the case was dismissed,
and Crowley had to pay costs. Crowley went back to Paris to
report to Mathers, and declared triumphantly that 'the rebel
camp' had broken up in anarchy. Crowley wrote in the
Confessions: 'They issued various hysterical manifestos, distinguished by confusion of thought, inaccuracy of statement,
personal malice, empty bombast and ignorance of English.'
To justify the latter jibe he quotes the rebels as saying
'nothing shall effect our connection', and explains condescend-
ingly: 'The poor dears meant *affect*.' It can be seen that
Crowley was not yet ready to undertake six months of
purification and prayer.

The Abra-Melin ritual has to be started after Easter, and
since Crowley had a month or so to spare, he decided to leave
the scene of past humiliations and go abroad. At Mathers'
home he met two Golden Dawn members who had just
returned from Mexico. They made it sound an interesting
place; so he sailed for New York. By the time he reached
there, Easter was behind him, and another chance of meeting
his Holy Guardian Angel had been lost.

After three days of sweating in a heat wave, Crowley took a
train to Mexico City. At first he loathed the place—it seemed
totally inefficient, and it was almost impossible to find
anything appetising to eat or drink. But when he had rented a
house overlooking the Alameda park, and hired an Indian
girl to provide for his domestic and sexual needs, he began to

like the *laissez faire* attitude of the Mexicans. He obtained an introduction to a local magical order, presided over by an old man called Don Jesus Medina, who was sufficiently impressed by Crowley's knowledge of the Kabbalah to initiate him through all its thirty-three grades in a matter of weeks. Crowley also established his own magical order, the Lamp of the Invisible Light, and initiated Don Jesus. His Ritual of Self Initiation involved 'the working up of spiritual enthusiasm by means of a magical dance' which induced giddiness. Crowley claimed:

> I used to set my will against the tendency to giddiness and thus postpone as long as possible the final physical intoxication. In this way I lost consciousness at a moment when I was wholly absorbed in aspiration. Thus, instead of falling into a dull darkness, I emerged into a lucid state, in which I was purged of personality and all sensory or intellectual impressions. I became the vehicle of the divine forces invoked, and so experienced Godhead.

But he admits that his results did not aid his personal progress 'since I had not formulated any intellectual link between the divine and human consciousness.'

All this makes it clear that, in spite of his instability of character, Crowley had a genuinely deep interest in magic. Sixty years later, he would have undoubtedly been an enthusiastic experimenter with psychedelic drugs. As it was, he was fascinated by other means of 'altering consciousness.' He had learned enough from Mathers to know how to produce certain strange effects, and he indulged himself with enthusiasm. He claimed to have learned the trick of making himself invisible, although it was only partially successful, and his physical image in a mirror became blurry and faint instead of disappearing. But he was convinced that the real secret of invisibility is a form of telepathy which somehow prevents other people from noticing you. (The playwright Strindberg held the same belief.) 'For example, I was able to take a walk in the street in a golden crown and a scarlet robe without attracting attention.'

Even Crowley was aware that his real problem was that he lacked the personal dedication necessary to be a true magician —that is, an explorer of the outer limits of consciousness. 'I felt instinctively that my pious predecessors were wrong in

demanding the suppression of manhood. . .' His solution was
to wear over his heart 'a certain jewelled ornament of gold'
(presumably a magically-consecrated talisman) whose purpose
was to prevent him from thinking thoughts that might hinder
his magical operations. When he took it off, he was allowed to
think, and do, whatever he liked. It turned him, he admits,
into a kind of Jekyll and Hyde. He was rather in the position of
a person who wished to become a Catholic priest while at
the same time keeping several mistresses. It never seems to
have struck him that there was a fundamental self-deception
involved.

Symonds has a penetrating comment about Crowley at this
period of his life, and it goes to the heart of Crowley's
personality problem:

> He needed some strong or horrific experience to get 'turned
> on.' Most people are 'turned on' by sitting at home with a
> book, listening to music, or looking at a painting. Crowley
> needed his Mexican whore with the worn face before he could
> write his verses about Tannhauser. In this sense, then, I say
> that he lacked imagination. As the course of his life shows, he
> went to great lengths to be stimulated; he could never get
> enough of fantastic adventures; the message didn't come
> through otherwise.

The result is that Crowley's life produces on most readers
the effect of an endless breathless gabble like a recorded tape
accelerated to several times its proper speed. The effect of the
next four or five chapters of his *Confessions* is certainly that of
a vertiginous travelogue. Eckenstein arrived in Mexico, and
they went mountaineering together, climbing Popacatapetl at
a gallop, with an unhappy newspaper reporter—who had
expressed his doubts about their climbing abilities—hitched
between them. He went through Texas, which he found
barbarous and horribly commercial. He travelled from San
Francisco to Hawaii, and on Waikiki beach met a married
woman with whom he had a love affair, celebrated in a
sequence of poems called *Alice, An Adultery*. In spite of its title,
it contains some moving love poetry. And a long poem called
The Argonauts is the most ambitious he ever attempted, 'a lyric
poem in which everything in the world should be celebrated
in detail.' He admits that it was inspired by the American
passion for tall buildings and vast processions. It contains
some of Crowley's best verse:

I hear the waters faint and far
And look to where the Polar Star,
Half hidden in the haze, divides
The double chanting of the tides;
But, where the harbour's gloomy mouth
Welcomes the stranger to the south,
The water shakes, and all the sea
Grows silver suddenly.

It may sound more like Robert Service than Swinburne or Wilde, but it has an irresistable forward rhythm.

Crowley paused in Hong Kong to renew acquaintance with the mistress who had helped him defy the London rebels, but was shocked to find that she had used her magical robes to win first prize at a fancy dress ball. Disillusioned, he went on to Ceylon via Singapore and Penang. In Colombo, he found Alan Bennett sitting at the feet of a Hindu guru, to whom Crowley took an instant dislike. He persuaded Bennett to leave with him for the healthier climate of Kandy, where he rented a bungalow. And here, at last, he was to settle down to the study of a subject to which he could respond with whole-hearted enthusiasm: yoga, which he defined as 'a scientific system for attaining a definite psychological state.' The problem with magic was that Crowley was never quite free of the desire to attain his own ends and, in this respect, his 'guru' Mathers set a thoroughly bad example. But Alan Bennett— 'the noblest and gentlest soul I have ever known'—was a different matter. Towards Bennett, Crowley felt none of that persistent rivalry that characterised his relationship with other males (and made it practically impossible for him to maintain a friendship). So for the next few weeks he studied the techniques of yoga under Bennett's instructions and, according to his own account, succeeded in attaining the first state of trance, known as Dhyana, a state in which the percipient and the perceived have become one. Crowley had another motive for persisting in his yogic studies—he believed it could be used 'to produce genius at will.' The chapter in which he describes these ideas (twenty-nine) is one of the most interesting in *The Confessions*, and demonstrates clearly that, whatever his faults as a human being, Crowley was undoubtedly no fraud as a student of techniques for transforming consciousness.

By this time, Bennett had made up his mind to become a Buddhist monk. He and Crowley took leave of one another, and Crowley went on to India, where he intended to join Eckenstein for an attempt to climb K2, also known as Chogo-Ri. He hated Calcutta as much as Texas, and his comments about it reveal that he continued to regard himself as a simple-souled idealist:

> My cynical disgust with the corrupt pettiness of humanity, far from being assuaged by the consciousness of my ability to outmanoeuvre it, saddened me. I loved mankind; I wanted everybody to be an enthusiastic aspirant to the absolute. I expected everyone to be as sensitive about honour as I was myself. My disillusionment drove me more and more to determine that the only thing worth doing was to save humanity from its own ignorant heartlessness.

But apart from his disillusionment with the crowds in the cities, the craving for adventure was stirring again. Bennett was in a monastery on the south coast of Burma, and Crowley heard that the journey across the Arakan hills was 'reputedly so deadly that it has only been accomplished by very few men.' He and a companion sailed for Rangoon, then took a steamer up the Irrawaddy River to Mindon. But when the headman told him that the coolies refused to go because the journey was too dangerous, he and his companion hired a dugout canoe and went downriver. Crowley was in a fever from malaria, and felt that the jungle was speaking to him of the world beyond material manifestations, and sleeping under a tree, he felt himself embraced by its elemental spirit—'a woman vigorous and intense'—who kept him awake all night in 'a continuous sublimity of love.' As they continued downstream, the nature mystic spent the day shooting at every bird he saw. A duck that seemed unkillable so enraged him that he insisted on going ashore to stalk it; his shot missed and it flew downstream. Then the bird made the mistake of flying overhead, and Crowley shot it from below so that it fell with a flop into the river. The episode reveals that manic persistence that made him such a bad enemy.

He eventually located Bennett in his monastery, and spent some time there writing a sequel to *Jezebel*. He also wrote an invocation to Hecate, the goddess of the underworld, and claims that when he recited it, the goddess appeared to him in the form of Bhavani, the Hindu goddess who wears a necklace of skulls. He says the vision made him aware of the basic identity of all religions. After this, he sailed for India, where he wrote an essay called 'Crowleymas Day', explaining that the universe is basically Nothing; he adds modestly that it may be regarded as a fair sample of his genius.

In Delhi, in March 1902, he joined Eckenstein and four other climbers for the assault on Chogo-Ri; this is the world's second highest mountain, less than a thousand feet lower than Everest. (Crowley would no doubt have preferred to attempt Everest, but it was then forbidden to Europeans.) It was a risky venture, for Chogo-Ri was generally regarded as unclimbable. Crowley devotes more than fifty pages of the *Confessions* to describing the expedition, and the reader soon senses that he regarded it as far more than a mountaineering challenge. Crowley's lifelong problem was a failure to feel himself a fully fledged member of the adult community; the doctrinaire religion of his childhood had left him with a kind of permanent inferiority complex. This was the real purpose behind his travels, his adulteries, his persistent attempts to outrage the bourgeoisie: he was trying to escape his old personality, to shed it as a snake sheds its skin. The world's second highest mountain was a symbol of achievement. The conqueror of Chogo-Ri would become an international celebrity, and his sense of his own value would be permanently secure.

Regrettably, the attempt was a failure. The party began the ascent on 8 June 1902, and eight days later, they were at the foot of the glacier that led up into the mountain. The sheer size and majesty of the peak overwhelmed them. Crowley began to suffer from snow blindness and exhaustion, to counteract which he drank champagne. Before they could begin the final ascent, the weather broke. And although two other members of the expedition finally reached a point two hundred feet beyond that of any previous expedition, the mountain finally drove them back. One of the party began to suffer hallucinations and had to be sent back. The man who accompanied him stole the emergency rations. As Crowley lay in his tent, suffering from malaria and listening to the howling of the storm, an instinct told him that the weather had broken for good. In any case, they were exhausted. So, with the storm still raging, they packed and retreated down the mountain. Two months after they had set out, they were again down on the plain.

In mountaineering terms it was Crowley's first recorded defeat. And in personal terms, it might also be regarded as the point at which Crowley's life began to take a downward turn.

Four

The Chosen of the Gods

IT WAS winter when Crowley arrived back in Paris. He stayed at the apartment of a Cambridge friend, Gerald Kelly, who admired Crowley's poetry, and who had decided to become a painter. (He ended up as a president of the Royal Academy.) In a restaurant called *Le Chat Blanc*, where Kelly dined every evening, he made the acquaintance of a young novelist named Somerset Maugham, who took an instant dislike to him, but who, five years later, used Crowley as the central character in a novel called *The Magician*. This is how he descibes him:

> [Oliver Haddo] was a man of great size, two or three inches more than six feet high; but the most noticable thing about him was a vast obesity. His paunch was of imposing dimensions. His face was large and fleshy. . .

And in his preface to the novel, Maugham notes:

> In early youth, I was told, he was extremely handsome, but when I knew him he had put on weight and his hair was thinning. He had fine eyes and a way. . . of so focusing them that, when he looked at you, he seemed to look behind you. He was a fake, but not entirely a fake. At Cambridge he had won his chess blue and was esteemed the best whist player of his time. He was a liar and unbecomingly boastful, but the odd thing was that he has actually done some of the things he boasted of.

Maugham also tells how, many years later, Crowley sent him a telegram saying: 'Please send twenty-five pounds. Mother of God [Crowley's latest 'scarlet woman'] and I are starving.' Maugham, who was notorious for his meanness, ignored it.

Inevitably, Crowley hastened to call on Mathers. But the

autobiography is oddly reticent about what occurred, except to record that Mathers failed to return a bag and a fifty guinea dressing case that Crowley had left with him before he set out on his round-the-world voyage—the impecunious Mathers had obviously pawned them. Symonds is probably not far from the truth when he suggests that Crowley was hoping to be received as an equal, and looking forward to showing off his newly acquired knowledge of yoga and Buddhism, while Mathers was not in the least interested in talking to 'equals.' Two such outsized egos were bound to clash sooner or later.

In the *Confessions* there follows one of those typically weird stories that leaves the reader baffled and irritated; moreover, Crowley quotes it in the words of his first biographer, Captain J.F.C. Fuller, as if to avoid the responsibility for personally vouching for its truth. Kelly is alleged to have told Crowley that a girl of his acquaintance—he calls her Miss Q—had fallen into the power of a 'vampire.' Crowley was asked to tea with Miss Q and the vampire—a middle aged lady he calls Mrs M. Left alone with her, he sat by the fire looking at a bust of Balzac. An odd dreamy feeling began to steal over him, and something 'soothing and lecherous' moved across his hand; the vampire was bending over him and touching his hand with the tips of her fingers. Moreover, she had been transformed into a twenty-year old girl 'of bewitching beauty.' Recognizing that he was almost in her power Crowley casually replaced the bust on the shelf and began making small talk. Suddenly, the woman leapt at him and tried to kiss him; Crowley held her at arm's length and re-directed her own evil current back against her. The fair skin wrinkled; the flaxen hair turned the colour of muddy snow, and the vampire, now a hag of sixty, hobbled from the room.

But there were stranger things to come. Crowley was convinced that the vampire was a puppet in the hands of far stronger masters. Kelly's girlfriend happened to be a powerful clairvoyant, and she obligingly went into a trance, and described a house which Crowley recognized as that of Mathers. But the inhabitants were not Mathers and his wife Moina, but a sinister pair called Mr and Mrs Horos, two dubious 'messiahs' who had been sentenced to long terms in prison the previous year. Now it dawned on Crowley why Mathers showed no gratitude to his former disciple. His body had been taken over by the evil Mrs Horos, while Moina was possessed by the husband, who was at present serving fifteen years for multiple rape. And as Crowley agonised about whether to try to save Mathers, the clairvoyant warned him to leave things as they were. . .

This is the kind of story that makes the reader suspect that Crowley was basically a total fraud. In *The Great Beast*, Symonds tells many such stories without any kind of commentary, and so produces the overall impression that the book is written tongue-in-cheek.

Now the truth is that, although Crowley *was* capable of outrageous invention, his tales were—as Maugham points out—usually based on fact. We have to remember that 'magick' is basically the development of a 'psychic faculty' which enables a person to see below the surface of the normal reality. If pressed to be quite specific, Crowley would probably have admitted that he 'saw' Mrs M transformed into a twenty-year old girl in the same sense that he 'saw' the Hindu goddess Bhavani when he recited his invocation to Hecate: that is, he saw it with his 'mind's eye.' We should also understand that when he speaks of vampires, he is not speaking of the bloodsucking variety described by Bram Stoker. It is undoubtedly true that some people have the power to drain others of vital energy; we have all encountered those irritating people who seem to leave us absolutely exhausted. Crowley would have described these as unconscious vampires. He also implies that there are certain people who can exercise the same power consciously, like Mrs M.

Now it so happens that, where Mr and Mrs Horos were concerned, Crowley was not entirely wide of the mark. Their story is one of the strangest in the annals of psychical research, and is worth retelling briefly here. The 'evil' Mrs Horos was actually a rather talented American adventuress named Editha Salomon, who claimed to be the illegitimate daughter of Lola Montez and Ludwig the Second of Bavaria. She had been described as a Madame Blavatsky without the intellect, and she certainly seems to have been a woman of commanding personality and considerable charm. Like Madame Blavatsky, she was probably a mixture of trickster and genuine clairvoyant. Like many mediums, she was a vast woman, whose eyes were totally compelling. Her career, like that of Madame Blavatsky, had many ups and downs, including a couple of brief periods in jail. In 1897, when she was forty-eight, she met a man fifteen years her junior, Frank Dutton Jackson, a failed priest, and the two married and went into partnership in the messiah business. Their disciples (sceptics said their dupes) adored them. But would-be messiahs always arouse hostility, and the Horoses, as they called themselves, were often driven to move on. To do them justice it must be said that even if they did have more than a touch of charlatanism, they were often treated with undue harshness by the authorities. In New Orleans, for example, the police could find nothing worse to charge them with than being 'dangerous and suspicious characters.' Later, charged with fortune telling, they were sentenced to thirty days in jail.

Early in 1900, the Horoses arrived on Mathers' doorstep in Paris; they had taken a large furnished flat, and said they had come to help him with his movement. Mathers was greatly impressed by the knowledge of magic shown by Mrs Horos, and since Mathers was himself a considerable scholar, we may conclude that Mrs Horos was not entirely a fraud. Mathers later told Yeats:

> She is probably the most powerful medium living. . . At times she has been controlled by very great and high forces, but much more frequently by evil spirits.

She had convinced him of her genuineness by relating to him details of a private conversation he had had with Madame Blavatsky. And he believed he had spoken to Fräulein Anna Sprengel (the original founder of the Golden Dawn) through her mediumship. But when the Horoses left Paris, for Cape Town, they took with them some Golden Dawn rituals and books on magic that Mathers had lent them, which led the paranoid Mathers to decide they were common swindlers.

One year later they reappeared in London and set up a magical movement which they called The Order of the Golden Dawn the Outer, presumably making use of the 'stolen' rituals. They also rented a house at 99 Gower Street (where the *Spectator* later had its offices), and announced the formation of The College of Life and Occult Sciences, whose subjects included 'mental and magnetic therapeutics, psychology, clairvoyance, clairaudience, mediumship, materialism, thaumaturgic power and Divine Healing.' They had various teachers and healers on the staff, and gave courses of lectures at a reasonable fee of from six to twelve shillings a course.

They were also—as the subsequent court case made clear—practitioners of some form of tantrism or sex magic. They had inserted in various newspapers advertisements in which 'an educated, attractive foreign gentlemen' wanted to meet a lady with a view to matrimony. Many applied, and the Horoses selected, among others, three attractive girls called Vera Croysdale, Olga Rowson and Laura Faulkner. Olga Rowson—a twenty-six year old housemaid—was to tell how she answered the advertisement, and was taken out to tea by the dapper and attractive Theo Horos, who flattered her and tried to fondle her. Back at the house, she felt 'quite helpless', and allowed herself to be persuaded into bed with Mr and Mrs Horos (the latter posed as his mother), where she yielded up her person. But, like the other female neophytes, she seems to have had no regrets, and formed a strong attachment to the Horoses. So did sixteen year old Daisy Adams, who had accompanied the Horoses to London from Birkenhead (where they had stayed with her mother), and who seems to have lost her virginity in a peculiar manner, probably through the ritual use of a phallic object. But the loss of virginity was—it became clear in the court case—all part of the initiation ritual, as in certain modern witchcraft cults. Vera Croysdale and Laura Faulkner told similar stories.

It was Vera Croysdale who set the machinery of justice in motion by complaining that the Horoses had borrowed money and jewellery from her and seemed to have no intention of returning it. Two detectives called at Gower Street to make enquiries. What they saw there made them persistent, and they questioned the girls, who innocently divulged that they regularly took part in sexual rites. The Horoses scented danger and fled back to stay with Daisy's mother in Birkenhead, where they were tracked down and arrested.

The case caused a sensation. The Horoses seem to have had no real sense of their danger. After all, they were able to produce letters in court in which the girls testified to their warm affection for the Horoses. Although Horos was accused of rape, there can be no doubt that he was technically innocent; the girls were all perfectly willing, both before and after. The Horoses were shattered and incredulous when they were found guilty. Horos was sentenced to fifteen years in prison, Mrs Horos to seven. It was undoubtedly a major miscarriage of justice; the Horoses were really being imprisoned for immorality. And Crowley, who might have been expected to be on their side, was totally unsympathetic. He states in the *Confessions* that Mrs Horos had 'bolted with such property of [Mathers] as she could lay her hands on' (which was untrue), then goes on primly: 'In the following year she was sentenced to seven years penal servitude for outrages on young girls. She had in some way used the rituals of the Order which she had stolen from Mathers to entice them to their doom.' And in due course Crowley was able to combine his distaste for the Horoses with his resentment of Mathers in his extraordinary tale about Mathers being 'possessed' by the spirit of Madame Horos. It is another illustration of the 'nasty, petty, vicious louse' aspect of Crowley of which Regardie speaks. Confined in the Female Convict Prison in Aylesbury, Editha Horos was in no position to 'possess' anyone.

In the *Confessions*, Crowley himself shows some awareness of the deterioration of his character at the time, writing:

. . . my spiritual state was in reality very enfeebled. I am beginning to suspect myself of swelled head with all its cohort of ills. I'm afraid I thought myself rather a little lion on the strength of my journey, and the big people in the artistic world in France accepted me quite naturally as a colleague.

By 'the artistic world' Crowley means Auguste Rodin, who was impressed by a sonnet Crowley wrote about his controversial bust of Balzac, and who invited Crowley to come and stay at Meudon 'to give a poetic interpretation of all his masterpieces.' The result was *Rodin in Rime*, which contains such lines as:

The veil o' th' mist of the quiet wood is lifted to the seer's gaze;
He burns athwart the murky maze beyond into beatitude.

Crowley published the book privately and, well pleased with himself, returned to London. Reading between the lines of the *Confessions*, it looks as if he may have decided to leave Paris to escape from an artist's model to whom he had allowed himself to become engaged 'out of sheer lack of moral energy.' Then, still suffering from moral lassitude, he returned to Scotland. Boleskine, he discovered, had acquired a bad reputation in his absence, and locals refused to pass the house after dark, preferring to make long detours. Crowley plunged into boredom. He tried to dispel it with one of his juvenile practical jokes, writing to a society for the suppression of vice in London to complain that prostitution was unpleasanly conspicuous in the neighbourhood. The society sent an investigator, and in due course reported to Crowley that he could find no sign of vice in Foyers; Crowley replied on a postcard: 'Conspicuous by its absence, you fools!'

Still bored, he went to Edinburgh to look for a companion-housekeeper, and found a suitable woman whom he calls 'Red-headed Arabella.' But she was not able to come immediately. So when Gerald Kelly wrote from Strathpeffer suggesting that Crowley should join him, Crowley accepted with relief. Kelly's sister Rose was also present. She was a woman of some experience, which must have appealed to Crowley, who had no use for innocent virgins. She had been married and widowed, and had scandalised her family by subsequently getting engaged to two men at the same time and having an affair with a married man; to extract money from her family, she told them she was pregnant, and they gave her forty pounds for an abortion, which she spent on dresses. The family retaliated by putting pressure on her to marry one of the suitors. Rose felt herself thoroughly ill-done-by, and poured out her heart to Crowley. It aroused his 'Shelleyan indignation', and he immediately proposed to rescue her by offering her his name in matrimony. His intentions were not romantic; he explained that after the marriage, they could separate, and she need never see him again. But it would prevent her family from forcing her into marriage. Rose was delighted with the idea. The next morning they fled by train to Dingwall, found themselves a lawyer, and were married before breakfast. At that moment, Gerald Kelly burst into the office and, on learning that they were already married, tried unsuccessfully to hit Crowley. When he calmed down, it was decided that Rose should return to

Strathpeffer and Crowley should go back to Boleskine, which is what he had intended anyway. (He adds complacently: 'I have frequently noticed that interference with my plans ensures their being carried out with exactitude.')

Partly to silence local scandal, Rose and he decided that they would take a train to some remote hotel together and pretend to be on honeymoon. The journey was passed in embarrassed silence; Crowley was feeling trapped, and was uncharacteristically at a loss for words. Unable to face the clerk at the hotel, he left Rose to register while he went off to contemplate the sea and brood on suicide; when he returned, he found that she had unsportingly booked a double room instead of two singles. It began to dawn on him that she was in love with him, overcome by his generosity in trying to save her. It would have been a pity to turn down a girl who was willing to give herself to him. 'I was willing to propitiate physiology. . .' So he did. And the next morning, he arrived at the astonishing conclusion that he was also in love. From then on, 'the honeymoon was uninterrupted beatitude.' Rose turned out to be exactly what he wanted: a rather masochistic female who liked to be dominated:

> Once, in the first three weeks or so, Rose took some trifling liberty; I recognised the symptoms and turned her up and spanked her. She henceforth added the qualities of a perfect wife to those of a perfect mistress. Women, like all moral inferiors, behave well only when treated with firmness. . .

All the same, 'love filled the universe; there was no room for anything else.' They went on to Paris, where they met Moina Mathers on a bridge; Crowley insists that she had become a prostitute, but this sounds unlikely. After that, they went on to Cairo where, to impress his wife, Crowley suggested spending a night in the King's Chamber of the Great Pyramid. Servants escorted them to the foot of the Grand Gallery; then they went on alone. In the King's Chamber, Crowley lit a candle, and began to read the preliminary invocation of the Goetia. Soon he realised that it was not necessary to peer at the page at close quarters; the chamber was full of a pale lilac glow—the 'astral light.' Crowley put out the candle and read on by the magical glow. Then they composed themselves to sleep on the hard floor, and spent an uncomfortable night. When they woke up, the light had vanished.

After this, they sailed for Ceylon, and Crowley noted with satisfaction that Rose fascinated every man who met her, 'a Helen of Troy or a Cleopatra.' He wrote a series of love poems to her, *Rosa Mundi*, and felt relieved that his poetic genius was returning (he was afraid that domestic happiness had stifled it forever). He also tramped around the jungle, blasting off at anything that moved and leaving a trail of slaughtered birds and animals behind. On the shores of a lake, he decided to shoot enough furry bats to make himself a waistcoat. His first shot filled the air with flapping wings. But one of the bats landed on Rose, and he had some trouble detaching its claws. That night, he was awakened by the noise of a squealing bat. When he looked up he saw Rose, completely naked, clinging with her arms and legs to the wooden frame that supported the mosquito net. When he pulled her down, she bit and spat and squealed; Crowley had to shake her awake. 'It was the finest case of obsession that I had ever had the good fortune to observe.'

When Rose discovered she was pregnant, they decided it was time to turn their footsteps towards home. In Cairo, Crowley decided to change his identity yet again. He admits this with some embarrassment in the *Confessions*, blaming 'the intoxicated infatuation of my hymeneal happiness' for his decision to 'play a puerile part on the world's stage.' Lord Boleskine (as he had been calling himself since his marriage) proceeded to don Persian garb and pretend to be an oriental prince, Chioi Khan, 'being Hebrew for the Beast'. (It is at this point in the autobiography that Crowley informs us that his mother believed he was the Beast—number 666—in Apocalypse; this sounds like one of his spontaneous inventions.) Crowley also wrote to Rose's parents informing them that in future all correspondence must be addressed to 'Princess Chioi Khan', and when Mrs Kelly added an exclamation mark after the title, Crowley returned her letter unopened.

Now, at last, Crowley returned to the study of magic; a 'sheik' who taught him Arabic also—'on discovering that I was an initiate'—provided him with books and manuscripts on the Arabic Cabbala, and taught him how to eat live scorpions, lick a red hot sword, and run a stiletto through his cheek without drawing blood.

Chapter forty-nine of the *Confessions* begins: 'This chapter is the climax of this book.' He also regarded it as the climax of his life. It describes how he received the curious 'scripture' known as *The Book of the Law*.

The Crowleys took a flat in Cairo, and Crowley tried to conjure up sylphs (spirits of the air) by repeating the invocation that had produced such an extraordinary effect in the Great Pyramid. Rose failed to see them, but sank into a curious state of mind in which she kept on repeating: 'You have offended Horus', which puzzled Crowley, since her knowledge of Egyptian mythology was almost non-existent. He was baffled and rather annoyed when she proceeded to tell him how to invoke Horus, by methods that struck him as 'pure rubbish.' But when she took him into the Boulak Museum next door, and showed him a stele containing the image of Horus, in a form known as Ra-Hoor-Khuit, he began to be convinced. It began to look as if the Secret Chiefs of the Golden Dawn were trying to contact him—presumably with a view to making him their intermediary instead of Mathers. On 19 March, 1904, at midnight, he made the invocation according to his wife's instructions (he was now calling her Ouarda the Seeress) and was told through her that 'the equinox of the gods had come, that a new epoch in human history had begun, and that he was to form a link between solar-spiritual forces and mankind.' In other words, Crowley had been chosen as the new Messiah.

Rose told him that the messages came from an entity who identified himself as Aiwas, Crowley's Holy Guardian Angel—the spirit Crowley had been trying to invoke with the unfinished ritual of Abra-Melin the Mage. Now Aiwas told Crowley (through Rose) that he was to go into his workroom at precisely midday on 8, 9 and 10 April and to write down what he heard for the next hour. What Crowley heard, or so he claims, was a 'musical and expressive' voice dictating a message for mankind. The message began, somewhat obscurely: 'Had! The manifestation of Nuit.' According to Crowley, this meant 'Motion, the manifestation of matter.' It went on: 'The unveiling of the company of heaven. Every man and woman is a star. Every number is infinite; there is no difference.' 'Every man and woman is a star' means, according to Crowley, that every man and woman is unique and remarkable, while 'Every number is infinite' means that every individual is the Ultimate God. But this spirit of tolerance towards all mankind is contradicted by much of the text that follows, which is élitist—in fact, Nietzschean, in tone. 'These are dead, these fellows; they feel not. We are not for the poor and sad: the lords of the earth are our kinsfolk. . . Beauty and strength, leaping laughter and delicious languor, force and fire, are of us.' It sounds like an extract from *Thus Spake Zarathustra*, except for the Swinburnian phrase about delicious languor.

Crowley argues that *The Book of the Law* supplants all previous religions, and that, unlike other holy scriptures, it contains the proofs of its own authenticity within itself. This is a claim that is impossible to take seriously. Passage after passage sounds exactly like the Crowley of *The Tale of Archais* and *Rosa Mundi*:

> I am the blue-lidded daughter of Sunset; I am the naked brilliance of the voluptuous night-sky. To me! To me! Thou art exhaust in the voluptuous fullness of the inspiration; the expiration is sweeter than death, more rapid and laughterful than a caress of Hell's own worm. I am in secret fourfold word, the blasphemy against all gods of men. Curse them! Curse them! Curse them! With my Hawk's head I peck at the eyes of Jesus as he hangs upon the cross. . . Let Mary inviolate be torn upon wheels: for her sake let all chaste women be despised among you!
> Bahlasti! Omnedha! I spit on your crapulous creeds.

All this sounds too much Crowley in his best Marquis de Sade vein to be accepted as a communication from an extra-terrestrial intelligence. In a comment added later, Crowley makes the 'priest of the princes Ankh-f-n-Khonsu' declare that the study of this book is forbidden, and suggesting that it should be burned after a first reading. Charles Cammell took this so seriously that he burned the copy inscribed to him by Crowley. But it is hard to see why Aiwas bothered to dictate it if its study was forbidden; it sounds like another attempt by Crowley to stake its claim as a supernaturally-conceived scripture. And as a piece of sacred scripture, it often makes an unfortunate impression, like some parody of *fin de siècle* prose by Max Beerbohm:

Hold! Hold! Bear up in thy rapture; fall not in a swoon of the excellent kisses. Harder! Hold up thyself! Lift thine head! Breathe not so deep—die! Ah! Ah! What do I feel? Is the word exhausted?

His guardian angel also advised Crowley to 'take wine and strange drugs. . . and be drunk thereof', promising that 'thy death shall be lovely—whoso seeth it shall be glad.' In fact, following this advice was to be Crowley's ruination, so that his death was anything but lovely. But the suggestion is certainly in conformity with the central doctrine of *The Book of the Law*: 'There is no law beyond Do what thou wilt.' This seems to be an echo of Rabelais's *Gargantua*, in which there is an abbey that has inscribed above its door 'Do what you will' (*Fay ce que vouldras*), and this seems to be confirmed by the fact that the abbey is called Thélème, and *The Book of the Law* states: 'The word of the law is Thelema.' Crowley's guardian angel may also have had in mind Blake's lines from *The Everlasting Gospel*:

> Do what you will, this life's a fiction
> And is made up of contradiction

—an attitude which is certainly consistent with Crowley's moral philosophy. Yet echoes of Rabelais's sixteenth century anticlericalism sound as much out of place in this 'sacred scripture' as the reminders of Swinburne and Nietzsche. Symonds hits the nail squarely on the head when he writes:

> *The Book of the Law* lacks the numinosity or authority of prophetic writings; and its rebellious sentiments exude an atmosphere incompatible with the 'praeter-human intelligence' which Aiwas was supposed to be.

All this may seem to suggest that Crowley concocted *The Book of the Law* to stake his claim as Mathers' successor and the founder of Crowleyanity. Yet no one who reads Crowley's endless essays and commentaries on it can maintain such a view. Nothing is more obvious than that Crowley believed totally in *The Book of the Law* as some kind of supernatural inspiration, and as his chief claim to be remembered by future generations. The main problem for the average reader—particularly of *The Great Beast*—is that Crowley seems such an intolerable show-off that it is hard to believe anything he says.

But then, a biography like Symonds' leaves out a whole dimension of Crowley's life. (He makes a more consistent attempt at understanding in its sequel, *The Magic of Aleister Crowley*.) It is impossible to understand Crowley unless we grasp that, like Madame Blavatsky and Mathers and Yeats and Florence Farr, he took magic as seriously as Lord Rutherford took atomic physics. Literary commentators often make the same mistake about Yeats: that he regarded magic as a romantic exercise in suspension of disbelief. Yeat's magical notebooks reveal this to have been untrue; they go into overwhelming detail about magical procedures and symbols, and show that he continued to be obsessed by it long after he ceased to be a member of the Golden Dawn.

Crowley, for all his inclination to embroider the truth, undoubtedly obtained certain results—both at Boleskine and in Cairo—that convinced him that he had the makings of a great magician. It may be that these results were not at all what he supposed them to be; that when he thought he was communicating with his guardian angel or some ancient Egyptian god, he was only establishing contact with some loquacious disembodied intelligence whose only talent was telling Crowley what he wanted to hear. Those who find the idea of disembodied intelligences impossible to accept may prefer to believe that Aiwas, Horus and the rest were projections of Crowley's unconscious mind. Nevertheless the one thing that seems relatively certain is that they were not pure invention.

The most sensible hypothesis about *The Book of the Law* is that it was largely a product of Crowley's own mind, but that he received it in a way that convinced him that he was only the amanuensis. His central claim about the work is that it opens up communication with discarnate intelligences. But when he goes on to quote it on the subject of food, drink and lovemaking ('eat rich foods and drink sweet wines and wines that foam! Also, take your fill of love as ye will, when, where and with whom ye will!') and to explain that 'the emancipation of mankind from all limitations whatever is one of the main precepts of the Book', the reader recognises that Crowley really means 'emancipation from the Victorian limitations that made my childhood so miserable', and that *this* was the one limitation that Crowley never succeeded in escaping from. Because of this obsession with the Plymouth Brothers and their intellectual and moral limitations, Crowley based his personal religion on a premise that would not take in an averagely intelligent schoolboy: that since there is no such thing as sin, everyone should feel free to indulge himself as much as he likes. This might work if all human beings were highly intelligent and self-disciplined, but at our present stage of social evolution, it would obviously be a disaster. And the fact that Aiwas—or whoever dictated *The Book of the Law*—shared this disastrous misconception seems to indicate that his intelligence fell well short of the superhuman.

Crowley admits that he also had his misgivings. But these were not about the philosophical implications of *The Book of the Law*, but about his own adequacy to carry out 'a mission of such importance that the last event in the world's history of importance even approaching it was Mohammed's...' All the same, he lost no time, when he arrived in Paris, in writing to Mathers to inform him that secret chiefs had now appointed him as the head of the order. Mathers ignored it, and Crowley says 'I declared war on Mathers accordingly.'

Back in Boleskine, 'life passed like an ecstatic dream'—at least, until Mathers began to mount a magical attack. He succeeded in killing most of Crowley's pack of bloodhounds, and in making the servants ill. One of the servants suddenly became 'maniacal' and attacked Rose; Crowley drove him into the cellar with a salmon gaff and sent for the police. When Crowley finally evoked Beelzebub, the 'magical attacks' suddenly ceased. In July, Rose gave birth to a girl whom Crowley named Nuit Ma Athanoor Hecate Sappho Jezebel Lilith. To amuse Rose during her convalescence, he wrote an obscene novel, *Snowdrops from a Curate's Garden*. He also began to publish his many volumes of poetry in collected volumes, whose title page bore the imprint of the Society for Religious Truth. For Crowley, the real joke was that his jest contained more than a grain of truth.

One of Crowley's former companions on Chogo-Ri came to stay—a Swiss named Jacot Guillarmod. Crowley amused himself by spinning an absurd yarn about a dangerous breed of wild sheep called the haggis, and when, one morning, his ghillie burst into the room crying 'There's a haggis on the hill', they all rushed out into the rain and spent an hour crawling uphill through the heather with their guns at the ready. The joke was finally on Crowley when Guillarmod blasted away into the mist and shot the local farmer's prize ram. Guillarmod had the ram's head stuffed and mounted.

Guillarmod's purpose in coming to Boleskine was to persuade Crowley to go on another Himalayan expedition: this time to the world's third highest mountain, Kanchenjunga, merely a hundred feet lower than Chogo-Ri. Crowley agreed, but only on condition that he should be the leader of the expedition. According to Crowley Eckenstein declined to join them 'for various reasons', but according to Symonds, because Eckenstein declined to accept Crowley as a leader. No two accounts of the expedition could be more different than Crowley's and Symonds'; yet the weight of evidence seems to indicate that Symonds' is more accurate. According to Crowley's version, the ascent of Kanchenjunga would have been a perfectly straightforward matter if Guillarmod had not broken his agreement to regard Crowley as the leader. Once Guillarmod became a rebel, and began to disaffect the others, everything began to go wrong.

Symonds describes Crowley's view of Kanchenjunga as 'optimistic to the point of blindness.' The approach is barred by precipices down which swept continual avalanches. When Guillarmod studied the route Crowley proposed to take, he became convinced that it was impossible. He also claimed to be appalled by the brutal way Crowley treated the porters (over two hundred of them when the expedition started), and was convinced that this was the cause of the failure of the expedition.

Crowley had left Boleskine in early May and arrived in Bombay a month later. Guillarmod had found two more alpinists willing to join them and pay their share of the costs: two Swiss officers named Alexis Pache and Charles Reymond. Crowley had enlisted a young Italian hotel manager named Righi, who could speak Hindustani and Tibetan. After a two-week march through the valleys of Nepal, they began the ascent on 22 August 1905. Three days later, differences of opinion had already developed, when Guillarmod found that Crowley had failed to provide the porters with suitable footwear, and that some of them were expected to walk barefoot on the glacier. Guillarmod felt that the steps Crowley cut in the ice were dangerous; in fact, two days later, one of the porters lost his foothold on one of them, and fell to his death. Porters were now deserting in droves.

On 31 August, a number of porters descended from Crowley's camp and told Guillarmod they were tired of being beaten by Crowley and were leaving; Guillarmod succeeded in persuading them to stay by promising them that henceforth Crowley would not lay a finger on them. (Crowley himself flatly denies striking any porter.) Guillarmod and Righi decided that the only solution was to depose Crowley from the leadership of the expedition. When they arrived at Crowley's camp the next day, there was a furious argument. In his own account, Crowley falls back on his usual explanation that Guillarmod had become mentally unstable, and suggests that the rebellion was nothing more than the resentment of foreigners being led by an Englishman. Unfortunately, this was the beginning of the end. Guillarmod declared that he was withdrawing from his agreement to regard Crowley as the leader, and said he was taking his contingent back down the mountain to the lower camp—in any case, there was not sufficient room for everyone to sleep at Crowley's camp. Crowley claims he warned the 'mutineers' that they would be killed if they went down that night. Pache decided to join them, his excuse being that the porter had failed to bring his bed; it seems more likely that he was also anxious to escape from Crowley. Crowley warned him that he would be dead within ten minutes.

The accident happened as Crowley had foretold. There were six men on the rope—three Europeans and three coolies. A barefoot coolie slipped, dragging the next man with him. Pache and another coolie also slipped. Guillarmod and Righi tried to hold them, but it was impossible. Snow slipped from under their feet, causing an avalanche and soon they were also hurtling down the slope. Guillarmod was thrown into a crevasse, and succeeded in pulling the unconscious Righi from under the snow that covered him. But it proved impossible to dig the other men out of the snow. The other officer, Reymond, who was in Crowley's camp, heard their shouts and came to help with the rescue work. According to Crowley, Reymond told him he would call him if he needed help, which is hard to believe—surely it was obvious that they needed help if they were screaming? But Crowley, undoubtedly seething with resentment at the mutineers, turned over and went to sleep, no doubt muttering 'Serves them right.'

And now the two stories of the expedition diverge completely. According to Crowley, Guillarmod now recognized that his leader had been right all along, and became very friendly. Then Crowley gave orders to Righi about bringing down his belongings, and sent for more porters to dig out the corpses. Then he went off to Darjeeling. Guillarmod's story, as reported by Symonds, is that Crowley descended the mountain at dawn the next day, passing straight by them as if he failed to see them. Crowley says he heard voices, and shouted in reply, but received no answer. So he left the expedition. In fact, it seems fairly clear that Crowley simply deserted the expedition, leaving the mutineers to 'stew in their own juice.' He cabled an inaccurate account of the expedition to the *Daily Mail* in London, using to release his bile against the Alpine Club. Symonds comments: 'If it was Crowley's intention to make himself odious in the eyes of all mountaineers, he succeeded completely.'

What is so astounding here is the incredibly bad judgement that Crowley showed. As far as mountaineers were concerned, to fail to go to the rescue of colleagues in danger was the unforgiveable sin. But Crowley might have got away with it if he had pleaded—as he actually did—that it was some kind of misunderstanding, then hurried down the mountain at dawn to help in the rescue. By simply walking off the mountain he was guilty of dereliction of duty, and no excuse could then save him from being regarded as a 'cad.' Worse still, he then returned to Darjeeling, and withdrew most of the expedition's funds from the bank (they had been mostly supplied by the others) then wrote a series of self-justifying articles in an Indian newspaper.

The matter is important because it was symptomatic of Crowley's most fundamental weakness: his laziness. He admits in the *Confessions* that 'it is part of my character to rest on my oars when a spurt would take me past the post', but he manages to make it sound like some kind of modesty, the British gentleman's indifference to winning the game. In fact, it was a childish tendency to abandon any responsibility the moment he felt the first sign of boredom. He simply refused to do anything he didn't like doing, no matter how much inconvenience it caused to others. In a word, he was utterly spoilt. And in the long run, Crowley himself was the chief sufferer, for he acquired himself such a bad reputation that it surrounded him like an unpleasant smell. It was the Chogo-Ri episode that first revealed this fundamental weakness—his tendency to quarrel with most other members of the expedition. But it was the Kanchenjunga expedition that brought it into the open, and placed Crowley's feet on the downhill slope that would end with complete social ostracism.

In Darjeeling, Crowley had a 'brief but intense liaison' with a Nepali girl named Tenguft, and proceeded to study the Persian language, since he intended to visit Persia on his way back to England. After that, he spent some time as the guest of the Maharajah of Moharbhanj and spent some time shooting bears and tigers—he was disappointed that he was not allowed to shoot elephants. He then wrote a pornographic treatise on mysticism called *The Scented Garden,* which he describes modestly in the *Confessions* as 'this spurt of genius'. All this, he admits, was in open defiance of the Secret Chiefs, who were anxious for him to get on with his major task: to bring the new religion to birth. When they picked him to do their work, 'they meant me to get busy and do it'; they wanted him to tackle the problem of his relation with the universe 'as seriously as the Buddha had done twenty-five centuries ago.' So they arranged to administer a sharp reminder. One evening in Calcutta, Crowley set out by himself to find a bazaar, and in a dark street, was attacked by a band of robbers in white robes. Fortunately, Crowley's hand was on his loaded revolver, so even as they pinioned his arms, he was able to pull the trigger. The men let go, and Crowley found himself free. Hurrying away from the dark alley, he recollected his earlier experiments in making himself invisible, and decided to try again. According to Crowley, it worked, and he was able to pass through the excited crowds without being noticed. In *The Great Beast,* Symonds quotes from the *Calcutta Standard,* whose headline read: 'Alleged Assault on European—Two Men Shot.' A reward of a hundred rupees was offered for the arrest of the European. Crowley only admits to firing one shot, but it seems more likely that, as was his custom, he blasted away wildly until the gun was empty.

The next day, 29 October 1905, his wife and daughter arrived; Crowley informed her that they were leaving immediately; offered a choice of China or Persia, she chose China, on the grounds that she was fed up with Omar Khayam. So they engaged a nurse for the baby, and fled.

They sailed for Rangoon, where Crowley left his wife and daughter in a hotel while he went to stay with Alan Bennett, with whom he discussed his spiritual quest. Then he and Rose sailed up the Irrawaddy to Mandalay. At Bhamo, an official kept him waiting for seventeen days for his passport, until Crowley went over his head and obtained the permission he required; in the *Confessions* he prints a long, sarcastic letter he wrote to the official, which reveals again that Crowley was inclined to nurse his grudges. Finally they crossed the frontier into China. It was a country that brought out some of Crowley's worst qualities. He explains that 'one cannot fraternise with the Chinese of the lower orders—one must treat them with absolute contempt and callousness.' And since these contemptible creatures respected a traveller insofar as he was overbearing, haughty and avaricous, Crowley had an excuse for behaving at his worst.

In Tengyueh, Crowley found another father figure—the British Consul, Litton, whom Crowley compares to Sir Richard Burton, and acknowledges that he learned more from Litton about China than he had learned in the whole of his previous life. But the relationship was brief—Litton soon died of some mysterious disease, possibly poisoned, and Crowley had the pleasure of flogging a Bengali doctor—'a burly nigger of the most loathesome type'—with a rawhide whip to force him to examine the body. They were able to reach no decision about the cause of Litton's death, and Crowley and Rose set off, surrounded by ominous rumours of native uprisings (it was the time of the Boxer rebellion) and murdered Europeans, for the Chinese interior. By this time the baby's nurse had run away with one of the muleteers, and Crowley had engaged a drunken Chinese interpreter.

Crowley's account of the 'walk across China' is a pleasant travelogue ('We crossed the Salween by means of a bridge ornamented with shrines and a delightful and romantically beautiful house for the toll keeper') punctuated by Crowley's opinions on aesthetics, Chinese cooking, opium and the stupidity of Europeans. He concluded that opium was a harmless and much maligned drug. 'The pictures drawn as to its effects are evidently coloured by the bias of the observer.' So he 'purchased the necessary apparatus' and learned to smoke it. On the day after New Year they crossed the Mekong into what is now Vietnam. Food was often scarce and they were occasionally forced to live for days on rice, Worcester sauce and dried milk. Crowley was disappointed that he had no opportunity to shoot a peacock. There was increasing friction between Crowley and his servants, which Crowley fails to explain, but which was no doubt due to his tendency to treat the Chinese with 'absolute contempt and callousness.' The interpreter, a Chinese named Johnny White, registered his own protest by riding off on Crowley's pony, which was considerable better than his own 'sorry screw.' It was the wrong thing to do to a man as touchy and vengeful as Crowley, who managed to catch up with him unperceived, while he was crossing a thorny hillside. Crowley jerked him into a large thorn bush, and left him struggling there while his own coolies rode past, administering a blow from his whip as each man passed. 'I had no more trouble of any kind for the rest of the journey to Yunnanfu', he records with malignant satisfaction.

By the time they reached Manhao, where Crowley was due to pay off his coolies, they were becoming 'mutinous'; he accordingly worked out a scheme to get his own back. Once he and Rose and their servant were installed in the boat, Crowley 'proceeded to pay the head man the exact sum due to him, less certain fines.' The coolies were enraged and called on the villagers to support them. As they faced 'thirty or forty yelling maniacs', Crowley ordered the Hindu servant to cast off the boat; understandably he was reluctant, so Crowley threatened to shoot him unless he obeyed. A few minutes later, Crowley looked back with satisfaction as the current carried him away from the infuriated coolies; it was the kind of triumph he relished.

En route to Hong Kong, Crowley decided that he and Rose would return to England in opposite directions; he would go via Shangai and America, while Rose could return via Calcutta and pick up their luggage. He mentions this decision in the *Confessions* in the most casual way, as if it was perfectly normal to leave one's wife and child in the middle of Asia. What he takes care not to mention at this point is that he was going via Shanghai to call on his ex-mistress Elaine Simpson—the one who had worn her ceremonial robes to a fancy dress party. As it turned out, Elaine, whose magical name was Sister Fidelis, lived up to her name and refused to be unfaithful to her husband. His guardian angel Aiwas, invoked by magical ceremonies, warned Crowley that Elaine would give him a great deal of trouble, and that he ought to break with her. Yet, paradoxically, Aiwas also advised him to make love to her, which seems to suggest that he was expressing Crowley's own desires. Frustrated and suffering from a bad cold, Crowley took a boat for Japan and Canada. He arrived back in England in early June, 1906, where he found letters awaiting him telling him that his daughter had died of typhoid in Rangoon.

Five

The Master and the Disciples

FOR CROWLEY, 1906 was a year of disasters. Soon after his return, he had to have an operation to remove an infected gland in his groin. Then he picked up a chill in his right eye, which required more operations, all unsuccessful. This was followed by neuralgia that continued for months. Finally, an ulcerated throat laid him low for the rest of the year.

He had also discovered, rather too late, that his wife was a dipsomaniac—which enabled him to achieve the recognition that she was entirely to blame for the baby's death, having failed to sterilize the feeding bottle when drunk. He also reached the curious conclusion that Rose's mother was to blame for having allowed her children to drink champagne in childhood. So he 'took the hag by the shoulders' and kicked her downstairs. Symonds has the interesting remark:

1907. . . was the year that he 'went wrong'—or so he said during the 1920s in an anxious and melancholy period of his life. I think he meant that in 1907 there was still time for him to turn back. Rose had given birth to a daughter, Lola Zaza. He was thirty-two years of age. His roving boisterous past could be set aside as the *Sturm und Drang* period of his life. He had still a chance of settling down and getting on with the business of ordinary living; but he kicked his mother-in-law downstairs instead. . . and strode on, into the Waste Land, praising the immortal gods.

There is considerable penetration in this comment. Crowley's money was running out, so there were good practical reasons for settling down and thinking seriously about the future. But Crowley had become an addict, not to drugs or alcohol, but to magic. He had experienced strange mental states and extraordinary visions. He was convinced that he was aware of a whole dimension of existence of which ordinary people are ignorant and, on the whole, he was probably right. Moreover, since his experience in Cairo in 1904, he was also convinced that he was the Chosen One who was due to inaugurate a new era in the history of mankind. And since he was to be the new saviour, he had to become a kind of symbolic Everyman, and fling himself whole-heartedly into the experiences of this world:

> . . . the mission, in order to carry out for which I was incarnated, was a mission to mankind; and this must explain why, *pari passu* [at an equal rate] with my personal progress, I walked continually in the way of the world. My spiritual life was now therefore definitely duplex, and this fact must be kept in mind if my subsequent actions are to be properly understood.

This vision of his destiny had been confirmed in Shanghai, when he had invoked his Holy Guardian Angel. Aiwas ordered him to return to Egypt with Ouarda (Rose). 'There I will give thee signs. . . Thus you shall get real power, that of God, the only one worth having. Illumination shall come by means of power, *pari passu*.'

Another commentator on Crowley, Jean Overton Fuller, suggests that Aiwas was actually some demonic entity sent to tempt Crowley, and points out that the voice came from over Crowley's *left* shoulder—the left-hand path being the path of black magic. But it seems just as likely that Aiwas was the voice of Crowley's own unconscious mind (a suspicion reinforced by Aiwas's use of '*pari passu*'—not a phrase one would expect from an ancient Sumerian deity).

At least this enables us to understand why Crowley found the idea of domestic felicity intolerable. The avatar of the future religion, the chosen one of the Secret Masters, was treading the path of 'real power', the power of the gods. And in spite of lack of general recognition, he had no doubt whatever about his own stature; in fact, lack of general recognition only led him to praise himself more vigorously:

> I had become so accustomed to columns of eloquent praise from the most important people in the world of letters, which had not sold a dozen copies; to long controversial criticism from such men as G.K. Chesterton. . . People acquiesced in me as the only living poet of any magnitude. . . Yet hardly anyone

had read any of my work and the intrigues of my enemies had made it impossible for me to make myself heard. . .

So as his fortunes seemed to be in decline, he became more determined than ever to batter the world into a recognition of his genius. And it was at this point that Crowley received a visit from a soldier who had served in the Boer War, Captain John Frederick Charles Fuller who—amazingly enough—had read some of Crowley's work and decided he was a poet of genius. By way of publicising his work, Crowley had offered a prize of £100 for the best essay on it. Fuller was the only person who decided to compete. When the two men met at a hotel in the Strand, they found themselves immediately in tune. Fuller had been a member of the Rationalist Association, and took a Nietzschean view of the harmfulness of Christianity. Yet he and Crowley were united in detesting the Marxists and others who wanted social revolution. 'We felt ourselves to be leaders. . .'

But these views were still a long way from Crowley's notion of himself as the founder of a new religion. How Crowley persuaded Fuller to regard him as the successsor to Jesus Christ and Mohammed, as well as the greatest poet in the English language, is still a matter of mystery. We can only assume that Fuller was another example of that unique phenomenon, the English eccentric, who doesn't give a damn about the opinions of his fellow Englishmen. It was, in any case, a fair bet that none of his fellow Indian army officers would ever read *The Star in the West*, 'A Critical Essay upon the Works of Aleister Crowley', which appeared in 1907. Crowley remarks: 'The style of *The Star in the West* is trenchant and picturesque. Its only fault is a tendency to overloading.' This is an understatement. Here is the opening paragraph of the introduction:

At first sight it may appear to the casual reader of this essay, that the superscription on its cover [i.e. the title] is both froward and perverse, and contrary to the sum of human experience. This however I trust he will find is not the case and, as Ianthe, will discover that after the mystic union has been consummated, the beautiful daughter of Ligdus and Telethusa was as acceptable a young husband as ever wooed nymph on the shaded slopes of Ida.

This was clearly not a work that would produce a revolution in the current estimates of Crowley. Crowley accordingly failed to pay Fuller the promised £100.

Much of 1907 was spent wandering around the Mediterranean with a demented nobleman whom he calls the Earl of Coke and Crankum, and whom Symonds identifies as the Earl of Tankerville. The earl was suffering from paranoia, and believed that his wife was trying to murder him by witchcraft; he was introduced to Crowley in a chemist's shop where Crowley bought his alchemical supplies. 'My plan in such cases is not to undeceive the patient' says Crowley smoothly, and he proposed to teach the earl how to perform magic to defend himself. It seems clear that Crowley saw him as a heavensent answer to his own lack of funds; he suggested a 'magical retirement', and they crossed the channel to Paris, then went to Tangiers by way of Marseilles and Gibraltar. Crowley devotes a chapter of the *Confessions* to describing their adventures in Morocco. They returned via Granada, where Crowley had a passionate affair with a gypsy; the poem he wrote about it contains the memorable lines:

For your hair was full of roses, and my flesh was full of thorns.
And the midnight came upon us worth a million crazy morns.

Inevitably, the earl's paranoia turned against Crowley; but in the autobiography, Crowley forgets to mention this, as the description of his gypsy love affair leads him to speak of other loves who provided inspiration for his poetry. It was left for Symonds to unearth a revealing comment made by Lord Tankerville to Crowley before they parted on bad terms: I'm sick of your teaching—teaching—teaching—as if you were God Almighty and I were a poor bloody shit in the street.'

What is interesting about this comment is that it makes it clear that Crowley had a powerful compulsion to teach. This is something that is easy to forget as we read about his life, with its scandals and broken friendships and seductions. In fact, this is the trap into which most of Crowley's biographers have fallen, from Symonds onwards. Crowley's life becomes merely an outrageous story, a kind of moral fable about selfishness and depravity, like Bunyan's *Mr Badman*. And, as the present writer can testify, it is practically impossible to avoid being sucked into this particular whirlpool, if only because Crowley's life presents such an ideal opportunity for telling a good story. Yet the moment the reader turns to one of Crowley's own books—like his dictionary of ceremonial magic 777, written at about this time—it is to realise that, whatever Crowley's faults as a human being, he was undoubtedly totally serious about magic and mysticism. And that moreover, from his own point of view, there was a great deal of justification for some of his more 'disgraceful' actions. He writes:

> Fortunately we have learnt to combine these ideas [of mysticism and magic], not in the mutual toleration of subcontraries, but in the affirmation of contraries, that transcending of the laws of intellect which is madness in the ordinary man, genius in the Overman who had arrived to strike off more fetters from our understanding. . .

And quite suddenly, in a flash, it becomes possible to grasp Crowley's own vision of the world, and to see what he was aiming at. He felt that he had seen, and directly experienced, a Dionysian vision of 'beyond good and evil.' Nietzsche had seen the same vision, and horrified his contemporaries by denouncing Christianity and writing in praise of war. Nietzsche had once been overtaken by a storm in a mountain hut where a shepherd was slaughtering a goat, and the smell of blood and the bleating of the goat had combined with the crash of the thunder and the beating of the rain, so that he had written: 'Will, pure will, without the troubles and perplexities of intellect—how happy! how free!' But when such a vision is expressed logically, in a work like *A Genealogy of Morals*, with its denunciation of the weak, it becomes ugly and frightening. Crowley saw himself as Nietzsche's true heir—after all, Nietzsche had only died in 1900—and was determined not to be driven insane by that paradoxical vision. He found himself surrounded by people who did not even begin to understand the vision, in whose eyes he was merely a rather vulgar and unpleasant exhibitionist. So kicking his mother-in-law downstairs was more than a burst of bad temper; it was a symbolic gesture, like Rastignac shaking his fist in Paris and exclaiming: 'It's between the two of us now.'
While Crowley was quite determined to live out his life according to his Nietzschean vision, he also recognized that it

would probably involve a lifetime of misunderstanding and hostility. In his own eyes, this made him a kind of martyr. And this is precisely how Charles Cammell and Israel Regardie and Kenneth Grant have seen him. Admittedly, they manage to present Crowley in this light by concentrating upon his magical aims and glossing over the scandal. But it at least has the effect of presenting the other side of the picture, and showing Crowley as he saw himself. The reader who really wants to understand Crowley will have to practise the difficult exercise of switching from one point of view to the other.

Crowley himself was determined to master this art. This is why, on his return from Morocco, he wrote a series of hymns to the Virgin Mary. He explains:

> I simply tried to see the world through the eyes of a devout Catholic, very much as I had done with the decadent poet in *White Stains*. . .

And the comment that follows gives us a glimpse of the real calibre of Crowley's mind:

> I did not see why I should be confined to one life. How can one hope to understand the world if one persists in regarding it from the conning tower of one's own personality? One can increase one's knowledge and nature by travelling and reading: but that does not tell one how things look to other people. It is all very well to visit St Peter's and the Vatican, but what would be really interesting would be to know how they look to the Pope. The greatness of a poet consists, to a considerable extent, in his ability to see the world through another man's eyes. . .

If Crowley had developed this aspect of himself, he would certainly have become one of the great writers of the twentieth century; it was precisely this kind of restless intellectual exploration that turned Yeats into one of the greater poets of the age. Crowley, unfortunately, lacked this passionate obsession with ideas for their own sake.

It was also in 1907 that Crowley decided that, since the Golden Dawn refused to accept him as its natural leader, he would form his own magical order to supersede it. He called it the Silver Star—the Argenteum Astrum, or A.A. In the early days there were only two other members: the 'alchemist'

George Cecil Jones, and Captain Fuller. Crowley proceeded to write a series of 'scriptures' for his order, such as the *Liber Cordis Cincti Serpente* (Book of the Heart girdled by a Serpent) and *Liber vel Lapidus Lazuli*. They were not, he explained, dictated by his guardian angel, nor of his composition, but somewhere between the two.

Speaking of his decision to restore magic to its original purity, Crowley again has a passage that allows us a glimpse into his basic insights. He is speaking of the 'ordeals' that the neophyte has to pass through to become an adept, and his determination to re-establish their essence:

> I was at first ignorant enough of Magick to imagine that this could be done by the simple process of replacing sham formalities by real ones. I proposed, for example, to test people's courage by putting them in actual contact with the four elements, and so on, as was apparently done in ancient Egypt; but experience soon taught me that an ordeal, however severe, is not much use in genuine initiation. A man can always more or less brace himself to meet a situation when he knows that he is on trial. . .

But Crowley reached the interesting conclusion that all this was unnecessary; once a probationer had taken the oath 'to perform the Great Work, which is to obtain the knowledge of the nature and powers of my own being', he seemed to 'rouse automatically the supreme hostility of every force, internal or external, in his sphere'—in other words, that he would set into motion certain forces that would subject him to the 'ordeals.' This is a passage of central importance, for it reveals that Crowley's interest in magic was based upon an intuitive conviction that there are certain unknown laws of being which shape human existence, and that these laws cannot be cheated. (Jung's idea of 'synchronicity' is based upon the same intuitive insight.) Crowley's own ultimate failure seems to suggest that, in spite of this knowledge, he was unable to resist the temptation to cheat—that is, to take 'short cuts.'

Soon the Silver Star acquired another neophyte, a strange-looking youth named Victor Benjamin Neuburg. Jean Overton Fuller describes him as he was some years later:

> He was all head, the body being a slight affair as to its skeletal structure. . . Rich brown locks grew from above a broad

forehead surmounting finely chiselled, aristocratic Jewish features. But it was his eyes that were everything. They were in shadow from his brows and additonally screened by deeply hooded lids, but opened to disclose an astonishing quality of forget-me-not or celestial blue. . .

Crowley heard about him through Captain Fuller, and called on him in his rooms at Trinity when he happened to be in Cambridge. Crowley describes him as a mass of neuroses with 'lips that were three times too large for him.' But Neuburg was full of 'exquisitely subtle humour', well read, and 'one of the best natured people that ever trod the planet.' Neuburg had tried practising mediumship, and Crowley instantly divined that he had an extraordinary capacity for Magick. Neuburg was captivated by Crowley, and an unsuccessful attempt by the Dean of Trinity to ban Crowley from the college only strengthened his loyalty. When Crowley, tired of trying to keep Rose off the bottle, retreated to Paris, Neuburg went with him. Crowley made him the butt of a number of cruel practical jokes, including getting him paralytically drunk on Pernod, and persuading him to get engaged to an artist's model who was Crowley's own mistress. (Neuburg was shattered and miserable when Crowley told him the truth.) Then, in an attempt to force Neuburg into some kind of contact with the real world, Crowley dragged him on a walking tour through Spain where, because they were so badly dressed, they were mistaken for brigands.

Crowley also invited Neuburg up to Boleskine for a 'magical retirement.' In fact, Neuburg soon learned the Kabbalistic technique of 'rising on the planes', imagining one's astral body to be rising into the air and entering the astral realms. Neuburg attained remarkable proficiency in a fairly short time, confirming Crowley's suspicion that he was naturally gifted in Magick. In one of his earliest experiences, he encountered the angel Gabriel, clad in white, with green spots on his wings, and with a Maltese cross on his head. On another occasion he had a 'bad trip' and encountered a red giant against whom he was powerless, and who cut Neuburg to pieces and chased him back to his body. Crowley taught him the 'Harpocrates formula', through which he slew the red giant.

It must not be assumed that these descriptions are lies or

fantasies; innumerable practitioners of magic have experienced them, and there is such a basic similarity in all their descriptions that it must be assumed that there is an objective component in the experience. If we assume that what happens is entirely 'psychological', and has nothing to do with spiritual entities, then at least the experience is some kind of exploration of an inner landscape which is common to all of us. The easy assumption—that Crowley and other Golden Dawn members were simply playing a game of self-deception—is ultimately untenable. When we realise that Crowley was responsible for introducing Neuburg to these amazing realms of self-exploration, it becomes possible to understand why Neuburg regarded his guru with a kind of adoration. But there was clearly another bond: that Crowley was inclined to sadism, while Neuburg had masochistic tendencies. One evening, Crowley accused Neuburg of lingering among the Qlipoth, the harlots of the astral plane, and 'corrected' him by giving him thirty-two strokes with a gorse switch, drawing blood. 'He is apparently a homosexual sadist', wrote Neuburg in his magical diary[1] 'for. . . he performed the ceremony with obvious satisfaction.'

Crowley also beat Neuburg on the buttocks with stinging nettles; and since all this seemed to fail to make Neuburg suffer, he began to make coarse anti-semitic remarks. This upset Neuburg. 'It is the very limit of meanness to grouse at a man because of his race.' He describes Crowley as 'a cad of the lowest type.' And at the end of the ten day retirement, Crowley made Neuburg sleep for the next ten nights on a bed of prickly furze (another name for gorse), in a freezing cold room—Jean Overton Fuller believes that this is how Neuburg contracted the tuberculosis that finally killed him in 1940, at the age of fifty-seven. At the end of this twenty day ordeal, Crowley told Neuburg he had passed his probation, and would be admitted to the lowest neophyte grade (known as 10 = 1.) During this period at Boleskine, Neuburg met Rose, who was obviously far gone in dipsomania—Crowley claims she was drinking a minimum of a bottle of whisky a day.

1. Quoted extensively by Jean Overton Fuller in *The Magical Dilemma of Victor Neuburg* (1965); the episode is also described at length in *The Magical World of Aleister Crowley* by Francis King (1977)

Crowley goes to some length in the autobiography to insist that he was still deeply in love with her (he described their marriage as one long sexual debauch), and that their divorce in 1909—to achieve which he supplied her with evidence of adultery—was really for her benefit.

After the magical retirement, Neuberg accompanied Crowley back to London, and helped him prepare the second volume of *The Equinox*, a 'review of scientific illuminism', a 'periodical' (actually, a series of bulky volumes running to over four hundred pages each) which Crowley proposed to publish twice a year, at the spring and autumn equinoxes. They contain a mixture of verse, plays and ,'magical scriptures', and are generally regarded as Crowley's major literary (and magical) legacy. Volume two appeared a few days after the autumn equinox of 1909. After this, Crowley and Neuburg went off to North Africa for yet another magical retirement.

The retirement was to be devoted to 'Enochian magic'—a form of magic revealed to the Elizabethan occultist Dr John Dee through the mediumship of his 'scryer' (or seer) Edward Kelley. A series of invocations, or 'calls', were dictated to Dee and Kelley in an unknown language called Enochian, which sounds like gibberish: 'Madariatza das perifa Liil cabisa micaolazoda saanire caosago. . .'; their purpose was to summon up demons. Nineteen of these Calls or Keyes were dictated, and the nineteenth is designed to allow the magician access to thirty 'Aires' or aethyrs—these being spiritual planes or dimensions of consciousness. In Mexico in 1900, Crowley had explored the last two of these Aires through the use of the nineteenth invocation; now he set out to explore the remaining twenty-eight. If we can believe Crowley's own account of this 'magical working', contained in a document called *The Vision and the Voice*, he achieved a series of strange visions of angels, demons and other spirit entities. In the fifteenth Aire, Crowley was told that he had now been promoted to the grade of a Master of the Temple—the experience he had longed for ever since reading *The Cloud Upon the Sanctuary*; it meant that he himself was now one of the Secret Chiefs.

Most of these explorations had been conducted during the periods of rest between tramps across the desert of Morocco. Neuburg, who had now received the name Omnia Vincam

('I shall conquer all') had been made to shave his head, except for two tufts of hair on his forehead, dyed red and twisted into the shape of demonic horns. On December 3, 1909, Crowley and Neuburg climbed Mount Dal'leh Addin, near the village of Bou-Saada, and Crowley tried to enter the fourteenth plane or Aire. But there was some obstruction—he only encountered layer after layer of blackness. Crowley decided to call it a day, and they proceeded to descend the mountain. Then Crowley was seized by a sudden inspiration. He and Neuburg went back to the mountain top, and proceeded to practise an act of buggery, in which Crowley was the passive partner; they dedicated it to the god Pan. (In the autobiography, Crowley only says euphemistically that he 'sacrificed himself'.) After this, Crowley staggered back to Bou-Saada in a semi-mystical state in which 'all impressions were indistinguishable.' When he came to himself, on his bed, he found himself changed. 'I did not merely admit that I did not exist, and that all my ideas were illusions, inane and insane. I felt these facts as facts.' And when, later that evening, he tried the invocation again, the veils of blackness were drawn aside, and he was admitted into a circle of stones, which he soon recognized to be veiled Masters. The angel told him that he had spent his life trying to achieve fame, power and pleasure, and that now he had become one of these Masters, who were as lifeless as stones. In a sense, Crowley had died. (Jean Overton Fuller comments that when Crowley decided he had transcended the condition of ordinary men, he 'ceased to be completely sane.')

The next three Aires brought more revelations about the nature and duty of a Master. On 6 December, it was time for a magical task involving some difficulty and danger. Crowley had to cross a symbolic abyss between ordinary men and the Secret Chiefs and, in order to do this, he had to invoke the demon of the Abyss, Choronzon. For this purpose they wandered around Bou-Saada until they found a valley floored with fine sand. They constructed a circle of rocks, and nearby drew a triangle, killing a pigeon at each angle and sprinkling its blood. Protective 'names of power' were traced in the sand. Neuburg sat within the inner circle, while Crowley, who was to act as a kind of 'medium' for Choronzon, sat outside, within the triangle. According to Francis King, such an act is unique in the history of magic. Then Crowley repeated the invocation, and Neuburg repeated a magical oath. Things then quickly began to happen, although the various accounts leave some doubt about precisely what it was. A voice that sounded like Crowley's cried: 'Zazas, zasas. Nasatanda zazas!', the words with which Adam is supposed to have opened the gates of Hell. Then Choronzon appeared, and began to utter blasphemies. After this, Neuburg began hallucinating, and thought Crowley had changed into a beautiful woman he had known in Paris. She proceeded to tempt Neuburg, who resisted. Meanwhile Crowley, who was wearing a black robe and a kind of Ku Klux Klan hood, called out: 'I think that's all there is.' He was mistaken. The courtesan offered to lay her head at Neuburg's feet in token of submission, an offer he again refused. Then she turned into an old man, then into a snake. After this, Neuburg saw Crowley himself crawling towards him, begging for water; knowing this was another delusion caused by Choronzon, he refused. Neuburg then conjured the demon, in the name of the most high, to declare his nature; Choronzon replied that he didn't give a damn for the most high, but admitted that he was Master of the Triangle. Neuburg, becoming nervous, asked protection from Aiwas, but Choronzon replied that he knew Aiwas, and that 'all their dealings with him are but a cloak for thy filthy sorceries.' Neuburg was trying to write all this down—for Crowley was apparently in a trance—but as he did so, the demon succeeded in blotting out a small part of the magic circle with sand, and suddenly leapt inside, in the form of a naked man (presumably Crowley was still sitting in his yoga position within the triangle) and grappled with Neuburg. It tried to bite his throat, and Neuburg tried to stab it with a magical dagger. Eventually, he drove Choronzon out of the circle, and repaired the break with his dagger. The courtesan returned, but was again rejected. Choronzon begged to leave the triangle to get his clothes, but was refused. After trying unsuccessfully to make Neuburg admit that magic was all nonsense, the demon gave up, and 'was no more manifest.' Finally, Crowley wrote the word 'Babalon' in the sand with his ring. The tenth invocation was over. He and Neuburg then lit a huge fire to purify the place, and destroyed the circle and the triangle.

Crowley's note to the account states that he 'spoke. . . in spite of himself, remembering afterwards scarcely a word of his speeches', which seems to make it quite clear that Choronzon spoke through his mouth. This would seem to suggest that the naked man who wrestled with Neuburg was again Crowley himself. But this fails to explain Neuburg's other hallucinations. It seems fairly clear that something extraordinary took place on that afternoon of 6 December 1909.

Crowley and Neuburg resumed their march the next day, this time walking across open desert (so far there had been roads), ignoring warnings from officials about brigands. As they marched towards Biskra, they continued to 'call' the aethyrs. At the Royal Hotel in Biskra, too exhausted to write, Crowley dictated a letter to Captain Fuller, referring several times to 'dear, kind Victor', but also mentioning that he was having an awful job keeping Neuburg away from Arab boys for whose brown bottoms he had a 'frightful lust.' This is one of the few indications that Neuburg, like Crowley, was bisexual.

The episode of the fourteenth call had brought Crowley a profound insight, which was to dominate the rest of his life: the recognition that sex was one of the most effective ways of 'focusing the mind', and that therefore it could be used as an aid to magic. It may have been this insight that decided Crowley to break his vow to the Golden Dawn, and publish their secret rituals in the third issue of *The Equinox*. This was too much for Mathers, who hurried to London and filed an injunction to prevent publication. To Crowley's rage, a judge confirmed the injunction. Crowley promptly appealed, and also consecrated an Abra-Melin talisman to aquire the affection of a judge. It seems to have worked; at least, the appeal was successful, and the third volume of *The Equinox* contained the forbidden material.

But all this cost money, and Crowley was beginning to run out—even his chief disciple Neuburg was not a bottomless well. In May 1910, he was struck by an interesting idea. At the home of a Commander Marston in Dorset (the commander was obsessed with tom-toms, which he believed had an aphrodisiac effect on women) Victor Neuburg went into a trance, in the course of which he performed a ritual dance.

(He also correctly prophesied that there would be two wars over the next few years, one involving Turkey, one involving Germany, and that the wars would bring about the ruination of both countries.) Marston suggested that the dances deserved to be performed publicly, and Crowley scented the idea of making money. A few weeks later, a performance was given at Crowley's flat in Victoria Street—this was to be a 'dummy run.' Crowley had recently acquired himself a new mistress, a half-Maori violinist named Leila Waddell, whose playing, according to Crowley, was 'coarse, crude, with no touch of sublety.' She was to play while Neuburg danced, and Crowley read his own poetry. Crowley had devised seven 'rites.' A young woman named Ethel Archer, whose verse had been submitted to *The Equinox*, later described that evening to Jean Overton Fuller. She and the rest of the audience sat on cushions on the floor, and were given a 'loving cup' that tasted like rotten apples, but which contained some drug which soon made them 'high' (the effect lasted for a week). Then Neuburg danced, while Leila played; Crowley claims she played like a master, and astounded the critics. After an impressive dance in which he whirled like a dervish, Neuburg collapsed on the polished floor. A highly favourable review appeared in the *Sketch*.

Now convinced that this was a paying proposition, Crowley decided to hire Caxton Hall, and charge five guineas for a series of 'Rites of Eleusis' that would take place on seven consecutive Wednesdays. Each evening would be dedicated to a rite based on one of the seven planets.

Crowley's description of the rite of Saturn sounds highly impressive, with symbolic dances taking place behind veils, while a voice recites verses from James Thomson's *City of Dreadful Night* complaining about the meaninglessness of life and advocating suicide. But this time the press was less favourable—notably, Horatio Bottomley's *John Bull* and a scandal sheet called *The Looking Glass*. The critic of *The Looking Glass* described how he was admitted by a 'rather dirty looking person attired in a sort of imitation Eastern robe' (probably Neuburg, who was notoriously averse to washing.) Then ghostly figures appeared on the stage, and a man who looked as if he had come out of a Turkish bath. The figure of 'the Master' appears, and the ghostly figures beg him to tell them if there is a God. The stage is plunged in darkness, and after a while, the Master returns and declares that there is no God, and that everyone should do as they like and make the most of this life. The writer then went on to hint that sexual irregularities probably took place in the darkness, and backed up his speculation by offering a potted history of Crowley. It referred to his association with a 'rascally Buddhist monk' named Alan Bennett, with whom Crowley had indulged in 'unmentionable immoralities', then went on to mention George Cecil Jones, and to imply that he had also had homosexual relations with Crowley. It seems likely that this scandalous gossip originated with Mathers.

Captain Fuller was thoroughly upset—after all, he had written a book about Crowley, and would now have to live down the imputation of being another homosexual. It was true that he was married, but then, so were Crowley and Jones. To Fuller's annoyance, Crowley declined to sue *The Looking Glass*. But Jones decided to go ahead on his own. The result was disaster, *The Looking Glass* insisted that it had not claimed that Jones was a homosexual, but argued that anyone who was closely associated with Crowley had no reputation to lose. A certain Dr Berridge, a friend of Mathers, appeared as a witness, and claimed that he had once asked Crowley if he knew that people thought he was a sodomite, and that Crowley had failed to deny it. Evidence of Crowley's indecent sense of humour was produced in court—such as the Latin marginal notes to an essay whose initial letters spelt piss, cunt, arse and quim. This finally convinced the jury that Jones had no case; they found that the allegation that he was a homosexual was true in substance and in fact. Captain Fuller was so upset that he broke off his friendship with Crowley. Recruitment to the Silver Star, which had been progressing healthily, now began to fall off. For the first time, the general public became aware of Crowley as a man of sinister reputation. For years Crowley had been out to shock and outrage the English, with absolutely no effect. One senses from his poetry and short stories that he often felt that any kind of notoriety was preferable to total lack of recognition. It must have been a startling experience to realise that his message was suddenly getting across, and that the notoriety was not an unmixed blessing. From now on for the rest of his life, Crowley would be unable to escape a reputation for wickedness.

For the moment, however, he was unaware of the disadvantages of being regarded as unspeakable. When he heard that Epstein's monument to Oscar Wilde in Père-Lachaise had been covered over with a tarpaulin because the statue's penis offended the guardian of the cemetery, he launched a campaign to defy the puritans. Having distributed pamplets asking the public to come and support him at midday on 5 November, he hid in the cemetery until the gates were closed, then sawed through the cords holding the tarpaulin, and attached thin wires so that a good tug from behind a nearby tree would unveil the statue. In due course, the crowds arrived, but the soldiers Crowley had been expecting to find on guard were absent. The French authorities had decided not to expose themselves to ridicule, and Crowley's unveiling of the statue was an anticlimax. Later, when he discovered that the penis had again been hidden from sight (this time by a bronze butterfly) he sneaked into the cemetery and stole it, then walked into the Café Royal in London wearing it as a codpiece, 'to the delight of the assembled multitude.' His craving for publicity was like an unquenchable thirst.

After this episode, Crowley and Neuburg returned to his 'beloved Sahara.' It was their intention to practise more Enochian magic and gain visions of the sixteen sub-elements, but Crowley found that, magically speaking, he was simply not on form, and gave up. He concluded that magic depends not on the conscious will, but on the 'true will', which may or may not be favourably disposed.

On 11 October 1911, Crowley attended a party at the Savoy given by the dancer Isadora Duncan for the birthday of her close friend Mary d'Esté Sturges, 'a magnificent specimen of mingled Irish and Italian blood', exactly the sort of extraordinary woman who always attracted Crowley. Crowley had recently learned that his ex-wife had been certified insane from 'alcoholic dementia', and was ready for a fresh adventure. Mary seems to have put up a certain token resistance, but when Crowley turned up at her Paris flat a few weeks later, she surrendered and accompanied him to Switzerland. Mary Sturges knew nothing whatever of magic. Retiring to bed one night after heavy drinking and some vigorous sex, Crowley was awakened by Mary, who seemed to be hysterical, and raved about some vision she had just experienced. She had seen a man called Ab-ul-Diz, who had spoken to her of matters she did not understand. Crowley finally recognized that Ab-ul-Diz was speaking in the language of magic symbolism, and that he knew Crowley's occult name, Perdurabo. (Crowley insists that Mary had never heard it.) Finally, Ab-ul-Diz announced that he would reappear in precisely one week, and took his leave. A week later, in the Palace Hotel in St Moritz, Ab-ul-Diz again appeared to Mary, and another magical conversation ensued. Mary was told that her magical name was Virakam; but otherwise, the exchange was frustrating and disappointing. But at least it seemed clear that, like Rose and Victor Neuburg, she was a natural 'scryer.' Subsequent encounters with Ab-ul-Diz led Crowley to believe that he was being ordered to go to Italy, and there write a book on magic. When he asked how he would recognize the place, a message flashed into his consciousness: 'You will recognize it beyond the possibility of doubt or error', and he saw a picture of a house on a hillside, with two Persian nut trees outside. And many days later, as they passed an overgrown lane in the car, Mary suddenly ordered the chauffeur to drive down it. When it seemed they could go no further, they found the villa with the nut trees. It was under repair, and the foreman told them it was not to let. But he proved to be mistaken; the owner allowed them to rent it for a small sum, and they moved in. And there Crowley dictated and Mary transcribed the work known as *Book Four*, one of Crowley's best and clearest expositions of the principles of yoga and his magical ideas.

One midnight, as he finished dictating, Mary was astonished when Crowley's face began to change, as if he was becoming a number of different persons in succession. Then the room filled with golden light, and Crowley's chair seemed to float off the ground and become a throne. Moreover, Crowley seemed to be dead. Mary fainted.

Book Four was intended to be in four parts; but after the second part, they quarelled—Mary seems to have possessed a violent temper—and rushed back to Paris. There she relented and telegraphed Crowley to join her, which he did.

But there were more quarrels, and soon she showed un-
mistakable signs of becoming an alcoholic. According to
Crowley, she then married a Turkish adventurer, who beat
her, then deserted her. Crowley felt, in any case, that a
magical partnership was out of the question. 'Her own
masterless passions could hardly have allowed her to pass
unscathed through the ordeals which are always imposed
upon those who undertake tasks of this importance.' Crowley
seems to have been a remarkably acute judge of other
people's characters; it seems strange that he displayed so little
insight into his own.

Six

The Magic Wand

EVER SINCE his vision of the fourteenth aethyr at Bou-Saada, Crowley had been dimly aware that there was some unfathomed connection between the two major interests of his life: sex and magic. The insight that was trying to break through into his awareness was that if sex is to be more than a merely physical activity, it demands precisely the same kind of mental disciplines as magic. At the time Crowley was attempting to form his own magical society to supplant the Golden Dawn, a Russian man of genius was organizing his first groups of followers in Tiflis and Moscow. His name was George Gurdjieff, and his central realization was that the human mind is appallingly feeble and undeveloped compared to the human body. We think that our lives have purpose and continuity, but this is only because the body is relatively durable. The mind that controls it changes from moment to moment. Our only chance of achieving any kind of real continuity is to make tremendous and sustained efforts of will. Gurdjieff's work consisted of various disciplines to make this effort possible.

By comparison, Crowley lacked profound insight into human nature; he wasted far too much time and moral energy fighting a rearguard action against the religion of his parents and grandparents. He never rid himself of the simplistic idea that the real aim of life is to enjoy oneself. Yet Crowley recognized instinctively that magic could offer some of the disciplines that his schooling had failed to instill. The way of the Kabbalah demands a high level of concentration and discipline of the imagination. Yet Crowley freely admits that he was too easily bored, and was always neglecting his magical disciplines. Like most of us, Crowley greatly preferred play to work. Tom Sawyer points out that work is what one is obliged to do and play is what one is not obliged to do. So as soon as Crowley committed himself to a discipline, the law of reverse effort impelled him to abandon it.

Now if there was one thing that Crowley preferred above all others, it was sex. And sex, by definition, was play. Yet that experience on Mount Del'leh Addin offered Crowley a glimpse of an amazing truth. Sex is also a discipline of the imagination. A man who makes love while thinking of something else will not really enjoy it. Conversely, a man who has spent a long time pursuing the girl of his dreams will treat lovemaking as a sacred rite; he will concentrate so as not to lose a single drop of the experience. Sexual pleasure depends upon a certain vital energy, but *the mind is the funnel through which this energy is poured*. Again, when a man is in bed with a girl in the dark, he has lost most of the visual aids that enabled him to appreciate her; the 'funnelling process' must include a certain capacity for *visualisation*—again, the same capacity required by a student of the Kabbalah.

What was slowly dawning on Crowley in the year 1911 was that sex could provide an easy and pleasant method of achieving 'magical concentration.' But at this stage it remained, as it were, in suspension, waiting for some event to crystallize it.

This event occurred in the following year, when Crowley received an unexpected visit from a German named Theodore Reuss, who introduced himself as a high-ranking German Freemason and the head of a magical order called the OTO— the *Ordo Templi Orientis*, or Order of the Temple of the East. And, to Crowley's astonishment, Reuss accused him of betraying the secrets of the ninth grade of this order. Now it so happened that Crowley *was* a member of the OTO—he had joined it in the previous year. But then, Crowley was a kind of collector of secret societies, and he had joined it thinking it was simply another order of Freemasons (otherwise, why did it call itself a temple?). Crowley hastened to point out that he had not reached the ninth grade, and so could not betray its secrets. Reuss then reached out and took from Crowley's shelf his recent work *The Book of Lies*, and pointed to a section that opened: 'Let the adept be armed with his magic rood and provided with his mystic rose.' Reuss was obviously unaware that although 'rood' means rod in old

English, it is generally used of a crucifix, and that this is what Crowley meant by it.[1] Crowley had a flash of intuition, and realized that the 'secrets' of the ninth degree were sexual in nature. He and Reuss had a long conversation about magic and sex, and found themselves in close sympathy. And when Reuss left, he had allowed Crowley to found an English branch of the OTO. Crowley had to go to Berlin to be initiated; typically, he chose for himself that magical name Baphomet—the name of the demonic idol that the Knight Templars were accused of worshipping.

The rituals of the OTO were not simply an excuse for sexual orgies. The order had been founded around the turn of the century by a rich German named Karl Kellner, and Reuss was his successor. (He seems to have been rather an odd character: a member of the German secret service, a journalist, a music hall singer, and a political agitator who tried to infiltrate the London Marxist organization.) Kellner had been heavily influenced by the branch of Hinduism known as Tantra, an attempt to achieve mystical union with the universe by regarding it as a continuous process of creation. This was blended with orthodox western magic, which is based upon the belief that the mind can exercise a direct influence on nature. One of the most widespread forms of magic, for example, is the charging of talismans with magical power—a talisman is a 'charm' designed to help its owner to achieve a certain end, such as wealth or sexual conquest or fame. A talisman would normally be 'charged' by the performance of a ritual of ceremonial magic. In the OTO, two 'initiates' would perform a ceremony culminating in a sexual act, concentrating on the aim of the magical operation, and end by anointing the talisman with a mixture of sperm and the secretions of the vagina, known as the 'elixir', or amrita.

Crowley's discovery of sex magic was indisputably the major turning point of his life. It united his two central aims: to be a magician and to be a sexual athlete. There was undoubtedly another aspect of Tantrism that attracted him. In

1 Symonds and Francis King point out that the Book of Lies bears the date 1913, but King argues convincingly that it was actually published in the previous year.

Tantric legends, most of its saints are initiated by a woman who is the 'power holder.' She might be a prostitute or a temple dancer, or some other form of 'untouchable', and one of the aims of uniting with her is to lose caste, to break all bonds with the everyday world. Crowley, with his strong masochistic tendencies, loved this idea of a female power holder, and it explains why, sexually speaking, his preference was for thoroughly experienced women like Rose, Leila Waddell and Mary Sturges.

Crowley must have deeply impressed Reuss, for Reuss not only agreed to allow Crowley to set up an English branch of the OTO, but seems to have accepted the basic tenets of *The Book of the Law*. (After losing this for several years, Crowley had rediscovered it in his attic in 1909, and had since become increasingly convinced that it was the Bible of the new religion that would replace Christianity.) Crowley's first act on becoming head of the London OTO was to rewrite all its rituals in his own inimitable style.[2] They are, of course, full of quotations from *The Book of the Law*, and laced with Crowleyan blasphemies, such as a section on the Black Mass in which Crowley attacks Roman Catholicism as 'that base and materialistic cult', and praises practitioners of the Black Mass because 'at least they set up Man against the foul demon of Christians.' When published in the German organ of the OTO, the *Oriflame*, Crowley's rituals caused some scandal among German members, and Reuss was heavily criticized. Even Reuss must have recognized by this time that Crowley was a man whose egocentricity knew no limits, and who would never be contented until he he had turned the OTO into an organization for the propagation of Crowleyanity. But before this could happen the First World War had broken out, and the problem was temporarily shelved.

But in 1913, it began to look as if Crowley had finally solved his financial problems with the help of magic and the OTO. He was charging a fairly high sum for initiation into 'its nine grades (£103. 10s) and thirty-three guineas a year membership fee. He had also succeeded in finding a theatre to present his

2. These have been published by Francis King: *Secret Rituals of the OTO* (1973.)

magical rites (the Old Tivoli) and under the name of the 'Ragged Ragtime Girls', they were a considerable success. There were seven girls, including Leila Waddell, and Crowley said they were three dipsomaniacs and four nymphomaniacs. In the summer of 1913, the girls were engaged by a Moscow theatre, and Crowley accompanied them. In a café he met a Hungarian girl named Anny Ringler, 'tall, tense, lean as a starving leopardess, with wild insatiable eyes', who had passed beyond the region where pleasure had meaning for her—Crowley means she was a masochist. Since he had a strong sadistic streak, they seemed made for one another, and they spent many idyllic hours in flogging and being flogged. It was Crowley's first experience of such a relationship, and for the next six weeks he wrote poems, plays, stories and magic rituals in a state of creative ecstasy.

Back in England, Crowley decided it was time to make full use of his newly acquired knowledge of sex magic. For this purpose, he and Neuburg went to Paris, and prepared to begin a long series of sex-magic rituals that Crowley would later call 'The Paris Working.' The 'working' began on the last day of 1913, when Crowley 'received the sacrament' (performed an act of sodomy) from 'the priest A.B.'—probably a journalist named Walter Duranty, foreign correspondent of the *New York Times*. Then Crowley painted a pentacle, a symbol of the god Mercury, whom they were trying to invoke, and Neuburg danced the 'banishing ritual', after which they invoked Thoth-Hermes (Mercury), and Crowley scourged Neuburg on the buttocks, cut a cross on the flesh over his heart, and bound a chain round his forehead. Forty minutes later, at midnight, the ceremony was concluded with an act of buggery, in which Crowley was the passive partner. Crowley records in his magical diary that he thought the room was full of snakes—symbols of Mercury, who has them entwined around his staff—while Neuburg was convinced that he was possessed by the spirit of the god. But Neuburg found it hard work, and failed to reach orgasm.

The following day, the ritual was repeated at the same time, and this time Neuburg succeeded in achieving an orgasm, and was so completely possessed by the god that Crowley was able to ask Mercury questions about how the rite could be improved. The rituals went on until 12 February and have been described at length by Symonds and Francis King.[3] At one point the god suggested that Crowley still suffered from sexual shame, and Crowley performed an act of sodomy in front of his friends at the house of his mistress Jane Cheron; his partner was Walter Duranty. One day, Neuburg became possessed by the god, and they were told that the supreme act of sex magic would consist of raping and murdering a young girl, dissecting her body into nine pieces, and offering them as sacrifices to various Greek gods. This was too much even for Crowley, and they decided to ignore it. During the thirteenth rite, the magicians had an insight into a previous life in which they had been together in ancient Crete—Crowley as a temple dancing girl and Neuburg as a young candidate for initiation; as a result of his failure to perform ritual rape on the dancing girl, both Neuburg and Crowley were sold into slavery. This revelation led Crowley to realize that he was unlucky for Neuburg; he might have gone further and reflected that he was unlucky for just about everybody he knew.

One of the aims of the Paris Working was to obtain money for Neuburg. In this it was apparently successful—a kindly aunt provided funds; but to Crowley's disgust, Neuburg bestowed the money on 'unworthy guests.' In fact, Neuburg was getting sick of Crowley. Jean Overton Fuller comments in her book on Neuburg:

> He [Crowley] did physical things, homosexual practices apart, of so revolting an order that I have thought it preferable not to repeat the examples I have been given.[4] [She adds:] He exploited others upon every plane, material, emotional and psychic.

And, it seems, back in London 'Victor was brave enough to see [Crowley]. . . and tell him he could go no further, and disavowed the oath he had taken at his reception into the

3. In *The Magic of Aleister Crowley* (1958) and *The Magical World, of Aleister Crowley* (1977) as well as in King's *Sexuality, Magic, and Perversion* (1971.) There is also a lengthy account in the 1971 edition of *The Great Beast*.

4. Symonds has no such inhibitions, and mentions the 'Serpent's Kiss'—drawing blood by biting the woman's wrist—and defecating on people's carpets.

Argentinum Astrum. Then Crowley ritually cursed him.'

Neuburg seems to have had another reason for breaking with Crowley; he believed that Crowley had murdered his (Neuburg's) mistress, Joan Hayes. She had been recruited by Crowley in 1910 to dance in his 'Rites of Eleusis' at Caxton Hall, having answered an advertisement in *The Stage*. Rebecca West, who knew her at this period, described her as an innocent girl, 'nice, stupid, very affected, good natured... with a tragedy ahead of her because of her ambition and her quite evident lack of gifts.' She was the type Crowley found completely unattractive, being anything but a 'scarlet woman.' But she was undoubtedly Neuburg's type, and Crowley seems to have been relieved when she married a friend of Neuburg's, Wilfred Merton. But the marriage did not last; six months later, Joan Hayes—now calling herself Ione de Forest—moved into a Chelsea studio and became Neuburg's mistress. Crowley was furious; he referred to Joan as 'Circe', and expressed the apprehension that she would seduce Neuburg away from the magical path. Neuburg and Joan Hayes took a cottage in Essex for weekends in the summer of 1912; two months later, she shot herself. In *Magick in Theory and Practice*, Crowley states that he 'once found it necessary to slay a Circe who was bewitching brethren. He merely walked to the door of her room and drew an astral T ('traditore') and the symbol of Saturn with an astral dagger. Within forty-eight hours she shot herself.' So it seems reasonably clear that, whether or not Crowley was responsible for her death, he certainly intended to be.

Crowley was in Switzerland when the Great War broke out, training for another attempt on Kanchenjunga; with some difficulty he succeeded in getting back to London via Paris. There, he claims, he tried hard to get some work serving the British government—phlebitis in his left leg made it impossible to join the forces. He was told he had no qualifications, even for the censor's office, so he decided to go to America, arriving in November, 1914. The war had put an end to his income from the 'Rites of Eleusis', and he was soon so hard up that he was forced to send back to England for some of his rare books and manuscripts to sell to an American collector, John Quinn. In the event, Quinn bought far less than Crowley had hoped. With no friends from whom he could borrow, no faithful disciples—like Neuburg—to exploit, Crowley found himself facing real poverty.

Before leaving England, he had started to keep a magical diary, with details of his operations of sex magic. On 3 September, he records that he possessed 'Marie Maddingley— respectable married woman' and adds: 'The girl was very weak, feminine, easily excitable and very keen, it being the first time she had committed adultery.' He records that the elixir—the mixture of male and female secretions, presumably drunk in an act of cunnilingus—was 'first rate.' Three days later, the partner was Peggy Marchmont, a Piccadilly prostitute, 'a sturdy bitch of 26 or so'. It seems clear that Crowley's powers of sexual endurance were considerable, for he records that the 'orgie' lasted from eleven in the morning to ten at night. 'I was not at all exhausted and could have gone on all night.' Oddly enough, the girl refused payment. On 14 October, ten days before he sailed, he performed a sexual 'operation' with a chorus girl, Violet Duval, assisted by Leila Waddell, though he does not explain what part Leila played.

In New York on 7 November, he was reduced to performing the sexual ceremony on his own, with his left hand, imagining Babalon (as he spelled it for numerological reasons), the Scarlet Whore. A week later, having sold the manuscripts to John Quinn, he was able to afford Elsie Edwards, an obese Irish prostitute who charged $3, but the 'unattractiveness of the assistant' made the operation difficult. On 21 November, the assistant was Florence Galy, the 'lowest type of prostitute, very negroid in type.' (Later, he adds that she is now in prison for theft.) After three weeks of solitary operations 'in manibus' (in the hand), he performed an 'orgiastic operation' with a Dutch prostitute, 'the muscular wolf type', who inspired him to magnificent efforts, although he complained that her secretions were not very plentiful and his semen was not properly dissolved therein. Crowley was becoming something of a connoisseur—he even refers to his sperm as being 'of excellent vintage'. But in a subsequent operation with the same girl, Crowley had diarrhoea, and had a premature ejaculation, and the elixir was of an acrid and aromatic type. He continued to perform operations with this partner through most of December and the first two weeks of January, although on 16 January 1915 he records an encounter with

'Margaret Pitcher, a young, pretty-stupid, wide-mouthed flat-faced slim bodied harlotry' with fair hair and a 'fine fat juicy Yoni'—this time the elixir was 'of pleasing quality'.

On 26 January Crowley met a widow, Lola Auguste Grumbacher, a Brazilian with a profile like Dante, admitting to thirty-seven years of age, and found her 'astoundingly passionate'. On the 26th she 'received the seed into her mouth' and so did Crowley. An hour later, she became so sexually excited that she was violently and repeatedly sick, which Crowley took to be evidence that she was possessed by the god Pan.

On 22 May, in the dimly-lighted steam room of a Turkish bath, Crowley was twice sodomised by strangers, and performed fellatio on another. A few days later, Crowley picked up another stranger called Finch, and was the passive partner in another magical act of sodomy. Finch invited Crowley to dinner with his wife (or mother it is not clear which) and Crowley seems to have attached great importance to this occasion, hoping that it might be some kind of breakthrough in his so-far disastrous American career. On the morning of the dinner, he even performed a special sexual operation with a young mulatto prostitute named Mamie, dedicating it to making 'a good impression on Mrs Finch and Co'. But the operation itself was a total failure. And, inevitably, the dinner was cancelled—perhaps because Mrs Finch discovered the nature of Crowley's relations with Mr Finch.

Crowley's account of all these magical operations make one thing perfectly clear: that the magic was not some kind of excuse for sex. For Crowley, magic was a religion, and he meditated on Hermes or Thoth as a Christian monk might have meditated on Christ or the Virgin. The man who had found the magic of the Golden Dawn rather boring and tiresome had now become a single-minded magician who thought and practised magic every hour of his life.

But on the day after the Finch fiasco, Crowley's period of frustration came to an end. A journalist friend invited him to dinner to meet two women, a poetess and an actress. The poetess was called Jane Foster, and she and Crowley were violently attracted to one another. The actress, Helen Hollis, 'glittered with the loveliness of lust', and was also apparently attracted to Crowley; but he much preferred Jane. The next

day, at her club, Jane proposed to divorce her husband and
marry Crowley. But she had to leave New York for a month,
during which time Crowley continued to perform magic with
prostitutes. When she returned, they became lovers; but she
proceeded to torment Crowley by telling him that she
detested the physical side of love (perhaps because he had
insisted on sodomising her). Then she left New York again. In
a state of misery, Crowley invited her rival, Helen Hollis, out
to lunch, then took her back to his apartment, and without
further ado, gave her a lengthy 'serpent kiss' with two teeth he
had had specially filed for that purpose.[5] The result was a
mutual 'surge of amorous frenzy', and after a twelve hour
orgy, he woke up 'purged of iniquity' and in a mystical state of
love. This experience somehow convinced him that he
should now produce a son who would also be his magical
heir, and on her return, he and Jane Foster laboured to this
end, apparently without success. What became of Helen
Hollis is not clear, she vanishes from the autobiography.

By now, Crowley had found himself employment—of a
sort. One day, sitting on top of an omnibus reading an English
newspaper, he was asked by an Irishman whether he believed
in a 'square deal for Germany and Austria.' When he replied
in the affirmative, he was invited to come to the office of a
newspaper called *The Fatherland*, edited by a man Crowley
had met in London: George Sylvester Viereck, a German-
American poet. Crowley, scenting employment, turned on all
his charm, and even threw in the falsehood that he was Irish;
Viereck promply hired him to write anti-British propaganda
for *The Fatherland*, directed at German-Americans.

Crowley's version of this discreditable episode is contained
in a lengthy chapter of the *Confessions*, in which he prints a
justification that he wrote a few years later. This justification is
that he was actually attempting to discredit German propaganda
by making claims so preposterous that no sane reader could
swallow them. *The Fatherland*, Crowley said, was learned and
logical; he would make it stupid and absurd. 'I worked up

5. An operation not without its hazards—Nancy Cunard
claimed that Crowley's fangs gave her blood poisoning after she
had rashly consented to a serpent's kiss without knowing what it
involved.

Viereck gradually from relatively reasonable attacks on England to extravagances which achieved my object of revolting every comparatively sane human being on earth.' But, he says, he did it with such cunning that the Germans never suspected he had his tongue in his cheek. It was a brave and noble sacrifice on Crowley's part—to allow his fellow countrymen to think him a traitor when he was actually working for the benefit of his country. He would have been saddened but not surprised by the lack of understanding of his motives. Years later, John Symonds wrote to Crowley's 'friend' Commodore Sir Guy Gaunt, director of British Intelligence in America, to ask if it was really true that Crowley was working for British interests in America. Gaunt replied:

> I think you describe him exactly when you refer to him as a 'small time traitor.' As regards his activities, I think they were largely due to a frantic desire for advertisement—he was very anxious to keep his name before the public somehow or other.

But he revealed that the British government was sufficiently worried about Crowley's activities to recall Gaunt from America to discuss what could be done; Gaunt urged that Crowley and *The Fatherland* were too unimportant to be worth worrying about. This view seems to be confirmed by the lack of impact of Crowley's other *Fatherland* publicity stunt: he and Leila Waddell (who had joined him in New York) took a motorboat out to the Statue of Liberty one morning, and Crowley made a speech renouncing England, proclaiming his willingness to fight to the last drop of his blood for Irish freedom, then tore up an envelope which (he declared) contained his British passport. Then Leila played 'The Wearing of the Green' on her violin. Crowley then sent a report of his gesture to various newspapers, but only the *New York Times* printed it. This gesture, Crowley explains in his *Confesssions,* was designed to win the trust of the Germans. The Hon. Everard Feilding saw the item in the *New York Times* and wrote Crowley a pained letter, but when Crowley replied explaining his true motives (to hoodwink the enemy) Feilding apparently 'understood and approved.' At least, so Crowley assures us; Feilding's view of the matter has not survived. Presumably as a result of his writings for *The Fatherland,*

Crowley had now made enough money to travel, and he proceeded to rush from New York to Detroit, Chicago, Vancouver—where one of his former disciples had set up a magical group—then to Seattle, San Francisco and Los Angeles. There he attempted to see Katherine Tingley, head of the American Theosophical Society, intending to propose an alliance, but his reputation had preceded him, and she declined to see him. He returned east via the Grand Canyon, which he found inferior to the Himalayas. Somewhere along the road back to New York he discarded Jane Foster, having decided that she was unworthy after all—he had come close to marrying her.

In New York he met the Indian writer on religion, Ananda K. Koomaraswamy, and lost no time in seducing his wife, a Yorkshire woman, who moved in with Crowley and became pregnant. Koomaraswamy apparently agreed to a divorce until his wife suddenly made a success as a singer (Crowley claims all the credit) and decided he wanted her back after all. But after a great deal more to-ing and fro-ing, she returned to England to have the baby, and had a miscarriage on the boat. Crowley was not too concerned about all this, for he was now in a state of immense excitement about a more important matter. The disciple in Vancouver—a man named Jones, known as 'Frater Achad'—had written to say that he had had a mystical vision, and that the Secret Chiefs had informed him that he was now ready to become a Master of the Temple, the same grade as Crowley himself. Crowley calculated that this happened precisely nine months after he and Jane Foster had tried so hard to beget a son. The conclusion was obvious. Although he and his mistress had failed, a son *had* been begotten in the magical sphere, and was therefore (presumably) ready to begin promulgating the doctrines of Crowleyanity, as prophesied in *The Book of the Law*. This also meant, of course, that Crowley had to move up another grade if he was to retain his superior position. In fact, Crowley had already awarded himself the supreme grade of Magus in the previous year (1915) and he now only had to ratify it with the correct magical ceremonies. This involved catching a frog, baptising it as Jesus of Nazareth, then crucifying it on a cross and stabbing it with a dagger. All this he did in the summer of 1916 near Bristol, New Hampshire and, having symbolically set himself up in the place of Christ, he gave himself a new magical name, Master Therion, or The Beast. Crowley might be unsuccessful in the worldly sense, but in the spiritual sense he was rising like a rocket.

In December 1916, Crowley went on a 'General Strike' against the Secret Chiefs, demanding some sign from them. Presumably this was successful, for by the end of January 1917 he was back in full swing with his sex magic, his 'assistants' including Sister, a 'big black muscular negro whore', Titusville Maddy, a prostitute, Anna Grey, and a man called Howard, on whom Crowley performed fellatio. In August he lived for a while with another Scarlet Woman, Anna Miller, a Dutch woman whom he called the Dog. Increasingly, the list of magical operations include the letters 'p.v.n', meaning *per vas nefendum* ('by the unmentionable vessel')—sodomy. When she became an alcoholic (a fate that seemed to overtake most of Crowley's mistresses) he got rid of her and began an affair with Roddie Minor, a 'big muscular sensual' matron, with whom the operations were also p.v.n. He called her the Camel. After her name, Crowley added the word 'Aphrodite'—meaning, as the editors of the *Magical Record* point out, that the muscular, sensual type was Crowley's ideal of feminine beauty.

Perhaps because Crowley encouraged her to take cocaine and opium, the Camel soon began having visions. She saw an egg full of convolutions of some flesh-like substance in a strange landscape, with a camel in the foreground. Then she encountered a wizard, an old man with a grey beard, dressed in a long black gown, who was infinitely wise. There was also a king who reminded her of a professor of her acquaintance. Crowley told the Camel to introduce herself as 'Eve', and ask the wizard's name. Instead of replying, he indicated that she had to build a fire of sticks. When she had done this, she saw a vision of a lion and a naked child. The wizard finally put his arm round her and told her: 'It's all in the egg.' So the vision ended.

More visions followed. Crowley was excited because the wizard (his name proved to be Amalantrah) was able to answer a 'test question' on the exact spelling and meaning of Crowley's magical name Baphomet; he said it was Bafometh, and meant Father Mithras. Moreover, the Camel's visions always seemed to involve the same landscape. 'There was,' says Crowley, 'what I may call a permanent background to the vision. He lived in a place as definite as an address in New York, and in this place were a number of symbolic images representing myself and several other adepts.' Jung had made a similar observation about his own curious visions of an 'underground world' in 1913,[6] and of an old man called Philemon. Jung had written: 'Philemon and other figures of my fantasies brought home to me the crucial insight that there are things in the psyche which I do not produce, but which produce themselves and have their own life.' In his conversations with Philemon, the old man said things which Jung had not consciously thought. Jung also observed that these 'visions' were accompanied by curious 'synchronicities', meaningful coincidences, and Crowley made the same observations. When he asked the wizard whether he could transpose his magical title 'Therion' into Hebrew letters, he was told that it was possible; he tried hard, but had no success in making the Hebrew equal the number of the Beast, 666. Two days later, he received a letter from some unknown Hebrew scholar which solved the problem—a letter which had been written at just about the time he was trying to solve it himself.

The Camel had a series of interesting visions, which are described in detail in an unpublished record, *The Amalantrah Working*. (Symonds gives a condensed version in later editions of *The Great Beast*.) They produce a strong impression that Crowley had discovered the key to the same mental 'underworld' as Jung, and that his excitement was justified. At the very least, Crowley's magical experiments may be regarded as an interesting development of what Jung called 'active imagination.'

Relations with the Camel began to deteriorate when Crowley met an attractive Russian woman called Marie Lavroff, whose resistance to his advances led him to call upon all his techniques of seduction. She held out for more than a fortnight, but finally, at midnight on 22 March 1918, joined Crowley and the Camel in an act of sex magic, designed to help Marie to transcend her 'sin complex' and to help the

6. See my *Lord of the Underworld*, pp. 74–6.

Camel to transcend her understandable jealousy. But two days later, after masturbating Crowley [which was apparently as far as she was willing to go] she fled, and the following operations of sex magic were conducted with the Camel alone. That summer, Crowley decided to go into another magical retirement, this time on Oesopus Island in the Hudson river. A writer friend, William Seabrook, managed to raise the money for Crowley's trip, as well as a canoe and a tent. When they went to see him off, they discovered that Crowley had spent every penny on tins of red paint and ropes—he told them that, like Elijah, he would be fed by the Ravens. Crowley used the ropes and red paint to print EVERY MAN AND WOMAN IS A STAR, and DO WHAT THOU WILT SHALL BE THE WHOLE OF THE LAW on cliff faces on either side of the river, where they could be seen from passing steamers. In fact, he was fed by neighbouring farmers. The Camel made a habit of coming to join him for weekends.

Crowley tells an amusing story that illustrates that, in spite of his increasingly bloated appearance and pointed teeth, he was still attractive to women. An artist friend in New York told him that he knew of a girl who was just Crowley's type, a redhead named Madelaine George. Crowley left a note at her hotel, inviting her to drop in for lunch on his island. To his surprise, he received a telegram a few days later asking him to meet her at the station. Crowley was disconcerted when she arrived with a huge trunk, and she was disconcerted to find that she was being taken to lunch in a canoe, and that instead of a mansion full of servants, Crowley possessed only a tent. She had hysterics and declared that she had to leave after lunch to see an imaginary brother. Crowley persuaded her to go for a row round the island, in the course of which the canoe sprang a leak and almost sank. After more hysterics and demands to be taken to the mainland, she decided to make the best of it and swooned into Crowley's embraces. She stayed for a long weekend.

Crowley was already involved with another 'scarlet woman' who would become something of a permanent fixture. One evening in the spring of 1918, a woman named Alma Hirsig— whom Crowley had met after one of his lectures—called at his Washington Square studio, together with her younger sister Leah. The latter was tall and thin, with luminous eyes, a wedge-like face, and a totally flat chest. 'She radiated an indefinable sweetness. Without wasting time on words, I began to kiss her. It was sheer instinct.' Leah seemed to enjoy it, and they continued kissing for the rest of the evening, occasionally coming up for air to make polite replies to the sister. Leah stayed the night. The next time the two called, Crowley punctuated the conversation by removing Leah's clothes, and asked her to come and pose for him—Crowley had started to paint while he was in America. In due course, he painted her as a 'dead soul', with a ghastly green face, surrounded by monsters. And she became his latest Scarlet Woman.

A subsequent 'magical retirement' on Long Island convinced him that his magical current was temporarily exhausted and that it was time to leave America. He stayed only long enough to supervise the publication of an eleventh and, it was to prove final volume to *The Equinox*, then, after a final night in the arms of the Camel, set sail for England.

Seven

The Abbey of Do-What-You-Will

FOR A PENNILESS exile, London in the December of 1919 was not a particularly welcoming place. According to Frank Harris (quoted by Symonds) Crowley left behind him in New York a string of dud cheques. He was hoping that the OTO would have money in the kitty, but soon discovered that the treasurer had embezzled it. He went to stay with an aunt in Croydon while he brooded on the future. His mind turned to Victor Neuburg, but his ex-disciple was nowhere to be found—in fact, he had read of Crowley's return in a newspaper, and was determined to avoid him. (He was living in Steyning and going through an 'Elizabethan period', dressing in breeches and leggings.) Crowley's health was poor; he was suffering from asthma and bronchitis, and the heroin and cocaine to which he had become addicted in America had lowered his resistance. A meeting with George Cecil Jones—the man who had introduced him to magic—was a disappointment; Jones had become a respectable bourgeois. After less than two weeks in England, Crowley left for Paris. There, a week later, Leah Hirsig joined him; she was pregnant with his child.

On 1 February 1920, he was cheered by what he took to be a sign from the gods. He called on an ex-mistress, Jane Chéron, hoping to smoke opium and make love to her. There was no opium and she refused to make love; but as he was leaving, she asked him to close his eyes, then presented him with a large square of cloth on which she had embroidered in silk the stele of Ankh-f-n-Khonsu, which he had seen so many years before in Cairo when *The Book of the Law* was dictated to him. She had made a drawing of it (from *The Equinox*) during a sleepless night, then decided to embroider it for him. Crowley was overwhelmed and he later referred to the event as a 'miracle'. It confirmed his belief that his steps were being guided by the gods. After anal sex with Leah, he noted in his diary: 'I am waiting without the least anxiety or eagerness for a new Current or a Word.'

He had installed Leah and her three year old son Hansi— by a former lover[1]—in a rented house at Fontainebleau. Now she told him that, on the boat from New York, she had met a French girl named Ninette Shumway, a widow who also had a three year old son and who was looking for a position as a governess. Crowley proposed that she should join them; his imagination was already toying with the idea of a *ménage à trois*. In fact, he was even dreaming of a *ménage à quatre*, for he was in correspondence with an American film star named Jane Wolfe, who had declared her passion for him by post, and with whom he was convinced he would fall in love at first sight—Crowley had a powerful streak of old fashioned romanticism. He went to Paris to meet Ninette Shumway, who proved to be a pale, tired-looking girl with a miserable child. She was obviously the type who could be dominated, so Crowley lost no time in sweeping her off to Fontainebleau. In his autobiography he tells how, on a May afternoon, they had lunch in a restaurant, then made love in the woods. But his magical diary shows that he was already performing sex magic with her within a few days of her arrival in mid-February. Shortly thereafter, he dreamed that he was inside a cave which he recognized as her vagina—a dream possibly inspired by the fact that she was trying hard to take him away from Leah. A few days later, Leah gave birth to a daughter, whom Crowley called Poupée.

Money was short, but Crowley was awaiting a cheque from his lawyer—probably an inheritance.[2] He was thinking about setting up an abbey modelled on Rabelais's Thélème, and spent some time looking at houses. He was probably grateful to get out of the house; having two wives was proving less delightful than expected, and he had to call upon every ounce of his pedagogic authority to convince them that jealousy was

1. In *The Occult* I state, mistakenly, that this child was also Crowley's.

2. Symonds mentions £3,000 inherited on the death of an aunt.

a childish emotion. The children were also a strain ('I am ready to bolt to some country where children are unknown'), but Crowley was unexpectedly patient with them. He tried asking the *I Ching*—the ancient Chinese oracle—where he ought to go. It was distinctively negative about Marseilles and Capri, but positive about Cefalu, the little port in northern Sicily. The *I Ching* also advised him to do nothing about an article in the magazine *John Bull* attacking him for his traitorous activities during the war; the oracle was undoubtedly correct. (Crowley relieved his indignation by writing the long apologia that appears in the *Confessions*, Chapter 76.) On 22 March 1920, he set out for Marseilles with Ninette and the 'brats', having despatched Leah to London to try to sort out his financial affairs. In Naples a few days later, Ninette was giving him trouble. 'A long, miserable night due to Beauty's sexual insanities.' Apparently Ninette had been something of a prude, and was shocked by Crowley's sexual demands. But she seems to have given way, for the following afternoon he records that she had taken part in an operation 'by the unmentionable vessel', and that it was orgiastic and prolonged. But he complains about being interupted by children. The following day, the money finally arrived, and he was able to go on to Cefalu.

The local hotel was so dirty that he swore he would not spend a second night there. At that moment, a man arrived who told them he had a villa to let. It was up a narrow path that wound its way up a mountain outside the town. The 'Villa Santa Barbara' resembled a run-down farm, but for Crowley it looked like a haven of peace: 'a well of delicious water. . . a vast studio opening northwards'. And there were two tall Persian nut trees outside the house, just as there had been in the earlier haven he shared with Mary Sturges. There was a magnificent view as far as Palermo and a garden full of flowers and fruit. The next day he clambered over the mighty rock of Cefalu, and visited temples of Jupiter and Diana; for dinner he ate thigh of kid and local sausage. It seemed a paradise. With his two wives and three children, the Master Therion felt he had at last come into his own.

The central hall was sanctified as a temple, in the centre of which stood an altar. Crowley soon covered the walls with pornographic paintings, one showing a man being sodomised by Pan, while his gushing seed covers a naked woman. But his aim, as he never tired of explaining, was to persuade people to take sex for granted, and stop regarding it as something thrillingly indecent—a notion that seems paradoxical, since this is obviously why Crowley enjoyed it so much. But it is a fact that visitors to the abbey were surprised that sex played so small a part in their lives.

Symonds makes the penetrating comment that Crowley was as serious about his magical religion as his parents had been about the Plymouth Brethren. In a sense, he was reverting to type. Life in the Abbey of Thelema was conducted on monastic lines, starting with a kabbalistic prayer and a ritual procession, followed by an adoration of the sun. This was all repeated at noon, in the evening and again at midnight. The children—who had ceased to snivel and become healthy, outdoor types—probably found it all rather like being at a Baptist school. The chief difference was that Crowley left piles of heroin and cocaine around, from which guests could help themselves. (He even tried practising sex magic under ether, and found that it heightened his consciousness of the whole operation.) On great occasions they performed the lengthy Gnostic Mass which Crowley had written for the OTO in 1913. The Communion involved 'cakes of light', whose recipe included menstrual blood. But life was not quite idyllic. Leah and Ninette were inclined to quarrel, and to Crowley's disgust, a quarrel broke out in the middle of a sex ritual to celebrate the entry of the sun into Taurus, and Ninette, practically naked, rushed out into the rainy darkness, so Crowley had to search for her. When he got her back, Leah was drunk and started another fight.

Crowley spent a great deal of time daydreaming about Jane Wolfe, who was now on her way to meet him. He had suggested that they should meet in Bou-Saada, scene of his vision of Choronzon, then changed his mind and telegraphed her to go to Tunis instead. He went there to meet her, but was unable to find her—she had failed to receive his telegram and gone to Bou-Saada. In his magical diary, Crowley frequently mentions his love for her. 'I adore her name. I hope she is hungry and cruel as a wolf.' On 18 June there is a long entry in which he vows total obedience to her. 'I am hers. . . I die that She may live. . . I drown in delight at the thought that I who

have been Master of the Universe should lie beneath Her feet,
Her slave, Her victim, eager to be abased. . .' But this thought
reminds him of his greatness:

> I am aflame with the brandy of the thought that I am the
> sublimest Mystic in all history, that I am the Word of an Aeon,
> that I am the Beast, the Man Six Hundred Sixty and Six, the
> self-crowned God whom men shall worship and blaspheme
> for centuries that are not yet wound on Time's spool. . .

His imagination was further inflamed by the cocaine which
he was taking in increasingly large doses. He was now an
addict, and spends pages writing about the effects of cocaine
in his magical diary. Sniffing it causes his nose to bleed.
Cocaine seems to have intensified his masochistic feelings,
and on 22 July he swore to take Leah as his high-priestess and
to act accordingly. And Leah, also half-insane with drugs, was
perfectly willing to assume the role; she ordered him to lick her
dirty feet, and Crowley obeyed. The following day, while he
was asleep, Jane Wolfe arrived at the Abbey of Thelema. She
was a shattering disappointment. Crowley seems to have
assumed that, because she had been a film star, she would be
beautiful; in fact, she was a battered, tough-looking lady of
about his own age. He compared himself to a girl who was
told she would meet a dark distinguished gentleman, and
found he was a one-eyed nigger. She had been attending
spiritualist seances and had received messages from various
'Masters'; Crowley read their messages, and was disgusted
by their asininity. 'During her first few weeks at the abbey,
every day was one long battle. I hacked through her barbed
wire of aggressive axioms. I forced her to confess the incon-
gruity of her assertions. I drilled holes in her vanity and self-
satisfaction.' Moreover, she was a highly moral lady, who was
shocked by the decor and the goings-on in the abbey.
Crowley decided that she either had to be subdued or ejected.
He told her that she should begin her training with a long
period of meditation—in fact, a month of it, in a tent on top of
the promontory, looking down on the sea. According to
Seabrook (whose account is based on her diary) 'she told the
Master Therion he was crazy. He told her there was a boat
touching next day at Palermo. . . and there was the open door.'
So, she accepted. During the next month she lived in the

tent, wearing only a woollen robe, eating bread and grapes brought to her by a boy. During the first few days she was nervous and uncomfortable, angry and resentful. Then she became 'calm but bored'. Then, after the nineteenth day, she suddenly plunged into a mood of 'perfect calm, deep joy, renewal of strength and courage'. Suddenly, she understood what Crowley had meant when he told her that she had the sun, moon, stars, sky, sea and the universe to read and play with.

Seabrook's explanation is that she had 'let go of herself' in New York, and 'gotten hold of herself' in solitude. But the truth is almost certainly the reverse. In New York she had become accustomed to stress, tension, endless hurry, until she had lost contact with her instincts, the 'forces of the right brain.' She had forgotten how to relax. In the tent, it gradually dawned on her unconscious mind that there was no need to hurry. Quite suddenly, her mind relaxed and her tensions dissolved away. It was a trick Crowley had first learned years ago on a long train journey from New York to Mexico City. He admits that he has always found journeys of more than half an hour tedious, and that even travelling from Edinburgh to Inverness he often felt on the verge of insanity. But after two or three days on the train, the boredom had vanished and he felt completely relaxed.

Since Jane was unsuitable (either for sexual or masochistic purposes) Crowley had to fall back on Leah. Two days after Jane's arrival, the diary contains a long entry in which Crowley bares his breast and admits his shortcomings. It seemed that:

. . .the first hour of my vow of Holy Obedience to Alostrael [Leah] proved Her to be the Scarlet Woman; she could have used her power in trivial ways; but She sprang instantly to Goddess-stature. . . First, She discovered the physical cowardice and dread of pain which I had sunk [i.e. buried] so deep by means of daring death-mountains. . . She held a lighted cigarette against my breast. I shrank and moaned. She spat her scorn and puffed at it and put it back. I shrank and moaned. She made me fold my arms, sucked at the paper until the tobacco crackled with the fierceness of its burning; she put it back for the third time. I braced myself; I tightened lip and thrust my breast against it.

Leah apparently saw through all his bluffs—saw that his erudition was a fake, that 'my worship was half pose, my miracle half craft'. She called his bluff and demanded the 'Eucharist'—that Crowley should eat her excrement, which lay on the consecrated plate on the altar. Crowley finally obeyed:

My mouth burned; my throat choked; my belly retched, my blood fled whither who knows, and my skin sweated. She stood above me, hideous in contempt. . .' [And he admits]: Simple enough, all this: in a word, I'm a Coward and a Liar.

The next morning, his tongue and throat were still sore.

The warm season was, on the whole, pleasant and peaceful, although drugs were weakening Crowley's health—he even had bronchitis in the middle of summer. Life with his concubines alternated between orgies of love and orgies of screaming—on one occasion Ninette threatened him with a revolver. The baby Poupée was sick—she had never been strong since birth. Oddly enough, Crowley had turned into a doting father. When the baby died in mid-October, he was shattered, and Leah, who was six months pregnant, had a miscarriage a few days later. 'I can only say that my brain was benumbed. It was dead except in one part where slowly revolved a senseless wheel of pain.' It was Leah who revived his courage and convinced him that he must live in the present, 'wholly absorbed in the Great Work'. He decided to go to Paris for a magical retirement. There he was overcome with grief, which became acute when he passed the hospital where Poupée had been born. But in the forest of Fontaine-bleau, 'the universal sorrow of nature flooded me and I broke out into strong sobbing.' Finally, the misery exorcised, he went back to Paris.

It was there that he met the mathematician and music critic J. W. N. Sullivan, who was travelling with a beautiful girl called Sylvia, a talented musician. Sullivan had acquired her from a literary critic, who had warned him that she suffered from one curious drawback; some lack of self-confidence that made her incapable of being happy. Sullivan had already discovered that this was true, and that it made their lives together oddly pointless. Predictably, Sylvia was fascinated by Crowley's powerful presence. He and Sullivan played chess together, talked all night, and discussed the law of Thelema; Sullivan ended by pledging himself to discover his True Will and to do it. Crowley then advised him to go off on his own to try and discover it, and rushed Sylvia off to his bed. He claims in the autobiography that Sullivan asked him 'point blank to take her off his hands for a time'. At all events, Sylvia became pregnant. As they made their way back to Cefalu, Sullivan demanded that Crowley return her, and Crowley, probably greatly relieved, promptly handed her over—to Sylvia's fury. Sylvia was to die shortly afterwards of typhoid, and Sullivan was to begin his writing career with a book in which he attempted to understand the meaning of the tragedy— the autobiography *But for the Grace of God*, which was to become a minor classic. He makes no mention of Sylvia's affair with Crowley.

Back in the abbey, Crowley's health continued to deteriorate and he suffered from boredom. He made an effort to break the heroin habit, and experienced constipation, sleeplessness and a return of his asthma.

The abbey now had a new recruit, a young American named Cecil Frederick Russell, who had read Crowley's articles for an American magazine and introduced himself to him in New York. Russell had been thrown out of the navy after taking forty grains of cocaine and trying to set a piece of glass on fire with will power. He had arrived just before Crowley left for Paris, and although Crowley welcomed him, hoping to seduce him—or rather, persuade Russell to seduce *him*—the new recruit proved to be more trouble than he was worth. Like Crowley, he had a pathological hatred of authority, and reacted with rage to anything that sounded like an order; he had attacked Leah twice in Crowley's absence. When another member of the OTO (Frank Bennett) was due to arrive, and Crowley asked Russell to give up his room, he met with a flat refusal. He finally had to order Russell to give up his room or leave the abbey—a sad expedient for a born anarchist like Crowley. When Russell's moods became a nuisance, Crowley suggested a magical retirement, and Russell hurried off to the top of the great rock of Cefalu and took a vow to starve for eight days. While there, he became convinced that he had been initiated into a higher grade than Crowley's, and came down more unstable than ever. They all heaved a sigh of relief when he finally left for Australia, even though Crowley reproached himself for his failure to cure Russell of his 'complex.'

By contrast, the case of Sir Frank Bennett was a triumph. Bennett was a Lancashire bricklayer who had joined the A.A. and the OTO, then emigrated to Australia. Now—like Sullivan's mistress Sylvia—he felt that he was totally unable to discover his True Will. The failure had profoundly depressed him. One day, as Crowley, Bennett and Leah were walking down to the beach, Crowley proceeded to expound his own Thelemite psychology. 'I want to explain to you what the Real Self is.' What he said was basically a variation on Freud. The subconscious mind is our true self, the Holy Guardian Angel, which experiences all that happens to us. It then does its best to persuade consciousness to act in accordance with its desires and needs; but consciousness, under the influence of society, is inclined to ignore or repress this advice. Sex is mankind's strongest need, and no amount of repression can prevent it from expressing itself. Freedom, said Crowley, consists in learning to stop suppressing the subconscious mind, and instead, learning to do its will.

For some reason, this simplistic and Freudian view electrified Bennett, who rushed downhill and plunged into the sea. After the swim, he asked in an awed voice: 'Please tell me again what you said just now.' Crowley had some difficulty in remembering, but finally succeeded. Bennett listened in silence, and when they came back to the abbey, went into a trance that lasted for three days. (This is Crowley's account; according to Bennett, he wandered about the mountain in a state of delirious torment before his mind grew calm.) Then he came to Crowley looking like 'an incarnation of pure joy', and told him that he had given him the key to the inmost treasury of his soul. What Crowley had done, said Bennett, was to teach him that doing his true will merely consisted in listening to the voice of his subconscious mind and doing what it directs. So, Bennett concluded triumphantly, Do what thou wilt shall be the whole of the law *is true*.

The reason for Bennett's excitement may not be immediately obvious; after all, Crowley had merely repeated the standard Freudian theory on sex, and had—in effect—told Bennett to 'let it all hang out.' But he had also grasped that Bennett's central problem was a confusion about the nature of his 'true will.' Bennett was a self-made man, a man who was used to taking conscious decisions and carrying them out. But he was also a deeply dissatisfied man, driven by a feeling that there had to be more in life than mere 'success'—hence his membership of the A.A. and the OTO. Yet the conscious will that had brought him material success seemed incapable of fulfilling his deepest needs. In telling him to listen to the voice of the subconscious, Crowley had shown him another way out: to stop willing and *relax*. It is unlikely that Bennett really went into a trance for three days. What is far more probable is that he was doing precisely what Crowley told him to do: sinking into a state of quiescence—like Jane Wolfe—and listening to an inner voice, of whose existence he had suddenly become aware.

So one man, at least, saw Crowley as he saw himself: as the great teacher and liberator. Bennett wrote in his journal:

> Twelve years ago I first saw the Beast, then I decided, half-heartedly, to follow him. But since I have seen him, and lived in the Abbey with him I have seen somethin' f his inner life; and his great disappointment, not with his work, but with those who ought to be carrying out his work. . . I am determined he shall not be disappointed in me; for I will spend the rest of my life in spreading his teaching. I may not be able to do much. But by the help of him, the Beast, and of my own Real Self, which he had given me an insight of—I may do much. For he alone led me to the knowledge of my real subconscious self. . .[3]

It is too easy to see Crowley as an overgrown juvenile delinquent with a passion for self-advertisement. But there *was* another Crowley, the Crowley recognized and admired by Frank Bennett. Unless we understand this, we totally fail to grasp the extraordinary influence that Crowley could exert on women like Rose and Leah, and on men like Neuburg, Sullivan and Bennett. They came to believe that Crowley was exactly what he claimed to be: a great teacher, the messiah of a new age. And this was not the gullibility of born dupes; Sullivan, at least, was one of the most intelligent men of his age (as his book on Beethoven reveals). Crowley *was*, in part,

3. Quoted in Symonds: *The Magic of Aleister Crowley*, p. 88

a great teacher, a man of profound insights. Mencius says:
'Those who follow the part of themselves that is great will
become great men; those who follow the part of themselves
that is small will become small men.' But Crowley was a
strange mixture who devoted about equal time to following
both parts of himself, and so became a curious combination of
greatness and smallness. A summary of his life, and his
extraordinary goings-on, makes us aware of the smallness;
but it would be sheer short-sightedness to overlook the
element of greatness that so impressed Bennett.

Other visitors to the abbey were Ninette's two sisters, Mimi
(her twin) and Helen, as well as the novelist Mary Butts, and her
lover Cecil Maitland. Crowley was impressed by Maitland's
intelligence, but made the penetrating observation:

> The great value of such men as Maitland and Neuburg to me has
> been to strengthen my conviction that in the absence of will-
> power the most complete collection of virtues and talents is
> wholly worthless. You must have a fulcrum, not only to move
> the world, but to move a feather.

Mimi was deeply impressed by Crowley, and only prevented
from joining the abbey by her middle class upbringing.
Helen, on the other hand, loathed Crowley and all he stood
for, without having the strength of personality to tell him so to
his face. She tried to influence the children—or 'corrupt'
them, as Crowley saw it—and when Crowley found out, he
ordered her to leave. Helen then went to the British consul in
Palermo and 'swore to a long list of lies.' But, claims Crowley,
she could only think of one thing that was actually illegal—
Crowley does not specify what it was—and the police called
at the abbey and could find no evidence. Possibly Helen had
complained about an act of intercourse between the Scarlet
Woman and a billy goat, which had culminated in Crowley
cutting the animal's throat—possibly because it had shown an
insulting lack of enthusiasm for the operation. Whatever it
was, it had the unfortunate effect of drawing the attention of
the law to the Abbey of Do-What-You-Will.

Crowley had spent the legacy that had enabled him to
move to Cefalu; now it was necessary to think of ways of
earning money. This would obviously be impossible in
Cefalu; so in January 1922, he went back to Fontainebleau.

Drugs had undermined his health, and the magical diary is full of accounts of his miseries. A disciple named Augustine Booth-Clibborn seemed to hold out a promise of renewed fortune, but he declined to sign Crowley's solemn pledge to undertake the Great Work—perhaps alarmed by Crowley's demands for money—and vanished. Crowley found Paris oddly disappointing. 'All the old enchantments had somehow vanished.' So he recovered some clothes he had left at the cleaners in 1914, donned highland costume, and set out with Leah for London. He had only £10 in his pocket, and was greatly amused when he was mistaken for a financier wanted for embezzlement and arrested near Boulogne; he was able to prove his identity by showing the police his photograph in Guillarmod's book on the Chogo-Ri expedition.

In London, his luck took a turn for the better. The novelist J. D. Beresford, the literary adviser of the publisher William Collins, succeeded in getting Crowley a contract for a novel to be called *The Diary of a Drug Fiend*. It was Crowley's first venture into commercial authorship, all his earlier books having been published at his own expense. He dictated the novel to Leah, who took it down in longhand, in twenty-seven and a half days, at a rate of just under five thousand words per day.

For a month's labour, *Diary of a Drug Fiend* is rather an impressive piece of work: the story of an ex-airman named Sir Peter Pendragon who becomes a heroin addict, and is saved by a meeting with 'Mr King Lamus' (Crowley) who invites him to his Abbey of Thelema at Telepylus, and cures him. It is unashamedly a *roman à clef*, and John Symonds' edition[4] has footnotes identifying almost all the characters. Pendragon is based on Cecil Maitland, and in the opening chapter, which takes place in the Café Royal, we meet Frank Harris, Lord Alfred Douglas, Augustus John, Jacob Epstein and many others, including Crowley, who introduces himself to Pendragon with the words 'Do what thou wilt shall be the whole of the law'—one of Crowley's more tiresome habits. Each of the characters is introduced with a thumbnail sketch. Mary Butts is a 'fat, bold red headed slut' who reminds the hero of a white maggot. Lord Alfred Douglas gives an impression 'of

4. Sphere Books, 1972.

some filthy creature of the darkness—a raider from another world looking about him for something to despoil', while the journalist T. W. H. Crosland is 'a huge bloated, verminous creature like a cockroach. . . his face bloated and pimpled, a horrible evil leer on his dripping mouth, with its furniture like a bombed graveyard.'

This acidulous way of descibing his characters is strongly reminiscent of Frederick Rolfe, 'Baron Corvo', the virulent, frustrated homosexual who wrote *Hadrian the Seventh*; it also has much in common with the method of Wyndham Lewis in novels like *The Apes of God*. And these comparisons are highly revealing. Both Rolfe and Lewis were bad novelists because they were so self-absorbed that they totally lacked the kind of objectivity that comes naturally to a born novelist; they were simply unable to get outside their own skins. Shaw once said that our interest in the world is the overflow of our interest in ourselves, and that until our interest in ourselves has been satisfied, we find it hard to pay attention to the world. Most people outgrow this stage in childhood or adolescence; but Crowley, like Rolfe and Lewis, never succeeded in satisfying the appetite, and remained in this state of self-absorption all his life.

Equally striking is the unselfconscious way in which Crowley can paint an immensely self-magnified portrait of himself in King Lamus (in fact, a character in Homer's *Odyssey* who rules over the cannibal giants, the Laestrygonians). Inevitably, Crowley produces the impression that, since nobody else is willing to blow his trumpet, he will do it himself. *Diary of a Drug Fiend* is an accurate measure of the immense, unsatisfied craving for recognition that dogged Crowley from youth to old age. It also explains why the British, when they finally became aware of Crowley, rejected him with such finality; his temperament was the reverse of everything the British admire. But for Crowley, the commissioning of the *Diary of a Drug Fiend* seemed a turning point in his life, the reward from the gods foretold by his guardian angel. And, to some extent, this view seemed to be justified. Collins accepted it immediately, and went on to commission Crowley's autobiography for an advance of £120—twice as much as they had paid on *Drug Fiend*. When *Drug Fiend* appeared, in November 1922— complete with a note explaining that the Abbey of Thelema really existed, and that the author would be glad to hear from prospective disciples—it was not greeted with the howls of derision that Crowley's smug self-portrait might have provoked. Critics found it a little too verbose, but gave Crowley high marks for good intentions in denouncing the use of heroin. When Crowley returned to Cefalu later that month, it looked as if he might anticipate a modest but continuous income from the use of his pen—he had also contracted with Collins to publish a series of stories about a detective called Simon Iff, and with another publisher to translate *The Key to the Mysteries* by Crowley's earlier incarnation, Eliphas Lévi.

Then the *Sunday Express* launched an attack on *Drug Fiend*; the author was James Douglas, the weekly columnist whom Lord Beaverbrook paid to be a kind of guardian of morality. He had already attacked Joyce's *Ulysses* and Aldous Huxley's *Antic Hay*, thereby greatly increasing their circulation (just as his successor, John Gordon, launched Nabokov to fame by denouncing *Lolita*). Crowley was not quite so lucky. The *Express* realized he was good copy, and the following Sunday followed up the attack with an interview with Mary Butts, describing 'profligacy and vice' in the Abbey of Thelema—she was presumably getting her own back for Crowley's attack on her *Drug Fiend*. The *Express* smacked its lips over stories of 'bestial orgies', and another friend of Crowley's, a woman named Betty Bickers—with whom he had stayed in London—revealed that he had borrowed money from her. Collins (Crowley's publisher) had been delighted with the James Douglas article, which could only increase sales. But the 'exposure' of the orgies and depravities was another matter; Collins published the Bible and other improving works, and to go on selling *Drug Fiend* after these attacks would be tantamount to profiting by the wages of sin. So they quietly allowed *Drug Fiend* to drop out of print.

Crowley's reaction to all this, in the final chapter of his autobiography, is typical; he finds the attitude of his publisher, 'inexcusable', and argues that the principles of fair play should be applied to 'cases which involve the suspicion of sexual irregularity.' The implication is clearly that he had been unjustly accused; Leah's copulation with the billy goat, and other similar episodes of sex magic, are conveniently forgotten.

In retrospect, it certainly looks as if Crowley had become the victim of a malign fate. He was correct to believe that *Drug Fiend* would mark a turning point in his life; but in his worst nightmares, could hardly have imagined it would be quite such a disastrous one. It is true that he might have taken warning from that earlier episode in 1910 when George Cecil Jones sued *The Looking Glass*, and the whole thing blew up in his face. But on that occasion, he had at least been more or less innocent. On the present occasion, he had provoked the attack by writing a vainglorious novel, and by using it as an opportunity to work off his malice against 'friends' like Mary Butts and Cecil Maitland. Mary Butts—actually a writer of considerable merit—may or may not have intended to ruin Crowley when she gave the *Sunday Express* interview; but Crowley's sketch of her as 'pompous, pretentious and stupid' and the author of 'the most deplorably dreary drivel' certainly gave her the right to aim a blow in return. As it happened, it went home with devastating accuracy.

Back in the Abbey, Crowley was not yet aware of the extent of the disaster. He was looking forward to the arrival of a new disciple, Raoul Loveday, a brilliant young Oxford man, to whom he had been introduced by Betty Bickers. Loveday had been studying *The Equinox* for two years before he met Crowley in the summer of 1922. Like Crowley, Loveday was a born anti-authoritarian. At Oxford, clambering over a wall to escape the proctors, he had transfixed his thigh on a spike and almost died. The same rebelliousness may explain his marriage to a Soho artist's model named Betty May, who had already been married twice before—Crowley says she was an alcoholic, a drug-addict and a prostitute ('an artist's model of the most vicious kind') as well as being brain-damaged; but then, Crowley had good reason to hate her. When Loveday was taken (alone) to meet Crowley, he stayed away for three days, and returned—by climbing a drain pipe—stinking of ether. For Crowley, it seemed that this was the disciple he had been seeking since the defection of Neuburg—intelligent, handsome (in a weak kind of way) and already devoted to the Beast. He lost no time in inviting the Lovedays to join him in Cefalu.

Betty May, who later described the whole episode in her autobiography *Tiger Woman*, was dismayed to find that the Abbey of Thelema was a grubby farmhouse without sanitation

or running water, and most of whose inhabitants seemed to
have an objection to washing. (Jane Wolfe had already
described Leah as 'filth personified.') Loveday, on the other
hand, was delighted with everything he saw; he described in
his diary waking the first morning to the throb of a tom-tom,
and joining the others on the olive-green hill for their
invocation to the rising sun. 'I cannot express my feeling of
exaltation as I stood there inhaling the sweet morning air. . .'
Then he and Crowley wrote all morning, and had a lunch of
meat, fruit and sharp Sicilian wine. In the afternoon they
climbed the great rock. When they returned, there was high
tea and a magic ritual, followed by a reading from Crowley.
Then talk, chess and mandolin playing until bedtime at nine.
For Loveday it was literally a magical idyll.

His wife found it all strange and nasty. She used to wash
naked at the pump in the early morning until she discovered
Crowley leering at her from round a corner. Observation of
the children soon convinced her they were spoilt brats—the
five year old smoked incessantly, and told her that he was
Beast Number Two and could 'shatter her.' Crowley allowed
them to witness the sex rites, believing it would keep them
free from repressions. No one in the abbey was allowed to use
the word 'I'—they had to say 'one'. For every transgression
they had to slash their forearms with a razor (there exists an
earlier photograph of Neuburg's slashed forearms). And
when Crowley did his dance of dionysian frenzy, Betty found
it impressive, but funny.

But Crowley and Loveday were ill of some liver complaint
much of the time (probably hepatitis) and medical attention
was less thorough than it ought to have been due to
Crowley's failure to pay the doctor. The climax came after
three months in an episode involving the sacrifice of a cat.
The animal had scratched Crowley when he tried to throw it
out of the room, and when he again found it in the scullery he
made the sign of the pentagram over it with his magic staff
and ordered it to remain there until the hour of sacrifice. The
cat did just that; it refused food, and when Betty May carried it
outside, it came back to the same place. Finally, the ceremony
was performed. Loveday, as a high priest, had to kill the cat.
Invocations went on for two hours, then Raoul took a kukri—
a big Gurka knife—and went towards the squirming sack on

the altar. When he slashed the cat's throat, it escaped and ran round the room howling. It had to be anaesthetised before Loveday could complete the sacrifice. Then Leah held a bowl under the throat to catch the blood. Crowley dipped his finger in the blood and traced the pentagram on Loveday's forehead, after which he handed Loveday a silver cup of the blood, which the high priest drained to the last drop. Loveday's enteritis later became worse, and he took to his bed. Crowley cast his horoscope and looked grim; he announced that it was possible that Loveday might die on 16 February, at 4 o'clock. Two days later, when he found Betty May reading a newspaper as she sat by her husband's bedside, Crowley snatched it from her—newspapers were forbidden in the abbey, on the grounds that 'having a library of first class books we should not spoil our appetites by eating between meals, especially the filth of the streets'. Betty began smashing things and threw glasses and jugs at Crowley's head; the sick Loveday had to stagger out of bed to defend his master. After that Betty left and went to a hotel; she had to be persuaded to return—after a promise of future good conduct. But Raoul's condition suddenly took a turn for the worst. At exactly the time forecast by Crowley, he died.

There was an impressive burial ceremony. Then Betty May left. Jane Wolfe also went to London, to try and raise funds and more disciples. And only nine days after Loveday's death, the *Sunday Express* carried a headline: NEW SINISTER REVELATIONS OF ALEISTER CROWLEY. Betty May described in details scenes of 'drugs, magic and vile practices'. *John Bull* followed up the attack, even accusing Crowley of cannibalism when in Kashmir. Crowley was ill in bed at the time—he had collapsed after the funeral. Now, perhaps feeling himself in need of moral support, he wrote off to another disciple, Norman Mudd, a young mathematical student who had unsuccessfully defied the Dean of Trinity on Crowley's behalf in 1909. At that time, Mudd had finally caved in to the pressure of the authorities, and had reproached himself for being a coward ever since. According to Crowley, 'shame dogged him by day and haunted him by night', and ten years after moving to South Africa, he had returned to England to search for the man who had impressed him so deeply. Hearing that Crowley was in America, Mudd had gone to Chicago, and succeeded in contacting Crowley's 'magical son' Jones, who had initiated him into the A.A. Now, at the summons of the Master, Mudd hurried to Cefalu eager to take over where Loveday had left off. He arrived on 20 April 1923.

A few days later, Crowley was summoned to the police station in Cefalu, and told that he had been ordered by Italy's new ruler, Mussolini, to leave Italian territory immediately. On 1 May, shadowed by a detective, Crowley and his Scarlet Woman left the Abbey of Thelema for Tunis.

Eight

Paradise Lost

THE SITUATION in which Crowley now found himself was one of almost grotesque irony. Ever since he had been a teenager, Crowley had believed that he was a great poet, an original thinker, a 'man of power'. The world had never shown the slightest sign of agreeing with him, so as time went by, Crowley's claims to genius became increasingly strident. He tried seriousness, he tried humour, he tried irony, he tried sarcasm, he even tried obscenity; the world continued to act as if he didn't exist. He published his collected works; he even published a book declaring himself the greatest man of his generation. *That* should have brought some response; in fact, it was hardly noticed. Yet writers like Shaw, Wells, Chesterton, and Yeats, seem to have had no difficulty whatever making themselves heard. There must have been times when Crowley felt like the invisible man. Even his most outrageous behaviour was ignored.

Then, all at once, the world noticed his existence—and reacted with a cry of disgust, as if it had trodden on a slug. It was like one of those fairy tales where the bad fairy grants a wish—but in a manner guaranteed to cause disaster. His craving to become known was granted in full measure—but at the cost of universal loathing. He was not even a 'figure of controversy'—like Ibsen or Zola—for he had no defenders. *John Bull* ran headlines like THE KING OF DEPRAVITY, A HUMAN BEAST and A MAN WE'D LIKE TO HANG, and the British public agreed with every word. It was also *John Bull* that coined the title that Crowley was to drag around like a ball and chain for the rest of his life: the wickedest man in the world. With a soubriquet like that, his chances of being taken seriously as a poet, a thinker, or even an anti-establishment rebel, were non-existent.

To say that Crowley had no defenders is not, perhaps, quite accurate: he had one, Norman Mudd. Mudd was a short, ugly, snub-nosed man who had lost an eye through a venereal infection, and he had been devoted to Crowley—in a dog-like, adoring way—ever since that meeting at Cambridge in 1909. He and Ninette stayed on at the abbey and Mudd wrote off letters to newspapers defending Crowley. In one of these, published in the Oxford student magazine *Isis* he asserts that Crowley's 'ideals are noble his honour stainless, and his life devoted wholly to the service of mankind'. He also calls Crowley England's 'greatest poet'. But he fails to explain why, if all the accusations against Crowley are 'baseless false-hoods',they came to be made in the first place.

Crowley had settled in a cheap hotel in the Arab quarter of Tunis. He had still not grasped the extent of his unpopularity. In any case, his attention was completely occupied by the problems posed by his addiction to heroin and cocaine; he was sleeping badly and vomiting, and had bad attacks of dyspnoea—difficulty in breathing. The magical diary lacks the usual entries on sex magic—presumably his health was too poor—and he was angry with Leah for refusing to wake him in the morning by getting into his bed and caressing him. He seems to be suffering from odd illusions about himself: 'If a man fucks a woman he admires her aesthetically... When a man fucks me I want to know it is for my beauty.' But he confesses to having lost interest in sex.

In June he made a remarkable attempt to break himself of the heroin habit—admittedly with the help of ether. He admits to having taken an average dose of three grains a day for more than two years. His 'cold turkey' treatment caused diarrhoea, vomiting, shortness of breath and delirium, but with impressive will power he persisted for three days, until on the fourth day he 'woke fresh, strong and well' and felt ten years younger. But two days later, he was back on heroin and cocaine. Much of the 'autohagiography'—as he liked to call the *Confessions* (a hagiography being the life of a saint)—was written under the influence of drugs.

Mudd arrived on 20 June 1923, and Crowley left him with Leah in the cheap hotel while he himself went off for a 'magical retirement' to the best hotel in Tunis, probably with money borrowed from Mudd. While he was there, the unexpected happened and Mudd and Leah fell in love. They told Crowley when he returned; Mudd even suggested marrying Leah, on the curious grounds that if she was his wife, she could then live up to her name of the Whore of Babylon by sleeping with Crowley. Crowley disagreed, and packed Mudd off to a 'magical retirement' in a nearby village. Crowley's sex desires were now reviving—perhaps because he had acquired himself a negro boy named Mohammed— and soon, he and Leah, with Mohammed in attendance, went off on their own magical retirement into the desert—hiring a camel for that purpose. Crowley and Mohammed performed sex magic; but when Crowley fell ill, Mohammed and Leah practised sex magic without his help. Finally, Mohammed and Leah fell ill too, and all three returned to Tunis. Crowley felt that his magical current was exhausted, for the time being. He wrote to the proprietor of a hotel in Paris where he had stayed before the war, assuring him that *The Diary of a Drug Fiend* had been an immense success, and that he would soon be able to pay the bill he had left owing in 1914; the proprietor agreed to allow him to come and stay on credit. So Crowley took whatever money was available—leaving Mudd and Leah penniless—and sailed off to Marseilles; he stayed in Nice with Frank Harris, who managed to borrow five hundred francs for Crowley's train fare, and then went on to Paris. There he stayed in the Hotel de Blois, and did his best to convince himself that all these adversities were part of the plan of the Secret Chiefs.

Mudd and Leah eventually managed to rejoin him in Paris by pawning Crowley's magic ring. When Frank Harris wrote to ask for a return on his five hundred francs, Crowley wrote him a long letter explaining why repayment was impossible, and then put before him 'the deepest conviction of his soul' that, rotten as he was in a thousand ways, he had nevertheless been chosen by the gods to inaugurate the new post-Christian era on earth. Capitalism, he said, was doomed, but Bolshevism was no real alternative. (Crowley had written to Trotsky from Tunis, asking to be put in charge of the extirpation of Christianity on earth, but had no reply.) The true answer lay in Crowleyanity, and if only Harris would become a Believer, his own troubles would be over. . .

Meanwhile, a new proprietor of his lodgings had decided

to evict him; Crowley pronounced a solemn curse, and soon after, the hotel went bankrupt. An effort to put a magical curse on Lord Beaverbrook and the *Sunday Express* seems to have been less successful. Mudd wrote a long open letter to Beaverbrook, and was despatched to London to distribute it. There he was forced to seek shelter in the Metropolitan Asylum for the Homeless Poor. Crowley, who always managed to fall on his feet, had meanwhile succeeded in borrowing money from friends like Sullivan and Jones, and was living fairly well in Paris. He and Leah moved to a hotel at Chelles-sur-Marne, and there he was sought out by yet another self-divided female in search of a Master: Dorothy Olsen, an American. Crowley lost no time in accepting her as a probationer of the A.A, under the name of Sister Astrid. It then struck Crowley that a Scarlet Woman with a bank account was a more logical companion for the future Messiah than a Scarlet Woman who was a financial burden. So he explained to Leah that the Secret Chiefs had ordained a magical retirement in North Africa, during which he should be accompanied only by Dorothy Olsen. When Norman Mudd returned from his unsuccessful attempt to rehabilitate Crowley in London, he found Leah penniless and half-starved. The two declared themselves married as a result of a private magical ceremony, and Leah became a prostitute to support her new husband.

Crowley was now on a three months magical retirement in North Africa with his new scarlet woman—who was presumably paying the bills. At one point a sheik recognized Crowley as a Secret Master and entertained him to a feast. But the strain of being a Whore of Babylon became too much for Dorothy, who began to exhibit the same signs of neurosis as Leah and other previous holders of the office—for example, abusing Crowley as a scoundrel. Yet when Dorothy found herself pregnant, Leah gave up her job as a potato-peeler in a restaurant and hurried to Tunis to help with the confinement; the journey proved unnecessary, for Dorothy miscarried.

And now, once again, Crowley's luck turned. His guardian angel had prophesied the arrival of a rich man from the west who would pour his gold upon Crowley. Now Crowley heard that Theodore Reuss, German head of the OTO, had resigned his position after a stroke. The acting head, Heinrich Tränker, had had a vision in which he saw Crowley as the head of a group of Secret Chiefs. He therefore wrote to Crowley, inviting him to a conference of the OTO in Germany. The fares would be paid by a wealthy member named Karl Germer. The result was that Crowley, Leah, Mudd and Dorothy Olsen set out for Thuringia, Crowley having sent a copy of *The Book of the Law* ahead of him. This was a rash move; when Tränker read its juvenile blasphemies, he was appalled; he thought the book was demoniacally inspired. Fortunately, Tränker then had another vision that changed his mind; he now declared that the book could be summarized in one word, civilization. Crowley's reaction to this curious assessment is unknown.

The German OTO was by no means unanimous in accepting Crowley as its new head. In fact, it finally split into three groups. One, led by Tränker, totally rejected Crowley. Another, led by a man named Eugen Grosche, accepted Crowley as an important teacher, but declined to regard him as a Secret Chief. The third, whose most important member was Karl Germer, swallowed Crowleyanity lock, stock and barrel. And for the next ten years or so, Germer continued to be Crowley's main financial support. As usual, the Beast had fallen on his feet.

Norman Mudd and Leah Hirsig now vanish from the story. When writing *The Great Beast* in 1949, John Symonds took the trouble to find out what had happened to them. Leah, he learned, had tried to live up to the doctrines of *The Book of the Law*—which she regarded as more important than Crowley— but was finally disowned by Crowley, who informed other members of the OTO to refuse all contact with her. She returned to America—whence her son had already been taken by sister Alma—and became a school teacher again. For this reason, Symonds disguised her identity under the name Leah Faesi in *The Great Beast*. She died in 1951. Norman Mudd also turned against Crowley, whom he believed to have betrayed the Secret Masters, and at one stage announced himself to be the new World Teacher. Symonds' enquiries elicited the fact that he had committed suicide on the channel island of Guernsey in June 1934, walking into the sea with bicycle clips on the bottoms of his trousers and the legs and pockets filled with stones.

Now once again solvent—thanks to Germer—Crowley installed himself once more in Paris. Symonds confesses with a sigh: 'A list of Crowley's mistresses at this time will get us nowhere.' But he quotes a letter from Karl Germer's wife to Crowley in which she complains: 'The $15,000 I have given you were spent not in real constructive work but in expensive cigars, cognac, cocktails, taxi's, dinners, wives and sweethearts, or anything you desired at the moment. . . God Almighty himself would not be as arrogant as you have been, and that is one of the causes of all your troubles.' It was a perceptive comment.

Like Norman Mudd, Crowley's 'magical son' Jones (Frater Achad) also began to suffer from delusions. He returned to England and became a Catholic convert—not because he had abandoned the doctrines of Aiwas, but because he hoped to convert the Catholic Church to the *Book of the Law*. Failing in this endeavour, he returned to Vancouver and was arrested for flinging off a raincoat and revealing himself naked underneath. Crowley expelled him from the Order.

In 1926, Crowley began to store up more trouble for himself by entering into correspondence with a young man from Philadelphia, Francis Israel Regardie, who had read Crowley's classic on yoga *Book Four*. Crowley advised Regardie to contact Karl Germer, who was now living in New York, and Germer sold Regardie a set of the *Equinox*. In October 1928, Regardie sailed for France to become Crowley's secretary. But his sister had meanwhile looked into the *Equinox*, been horrified by its attitude to sex, and begged the French consul to deny her brother a visa. This was impossible—it had already been granted—but the consul referred the matter to Paris for investigation. Meanwhile, Regardie arrived in Paris and was met by Crowley; he moved into a flat at 55 Avenue de Suffren with Crowley and his latest Scarlet Woman, a flamboyant Nicaraguan lady named Maria de Miramar. Crowley had also acquired another well-off disciple, Gerald Yorke; Regardie confesses that both he and Yorke were nervous in case Crowley tried 'some homosexual monkey tricks', but apparently neither had any reason for alarm. The French police, alerted by the New York consul, proceeded to investigate Crowley, and learned of his expulsion from Cefalu and of his drug-taking; in March 1929, Crowley, Regardie and Maria de

Miramar were ordered to leave France forthwith. Crowley managed to delay his expulsion by pleading illness, but Regardie and the Scarlet Woman had to leave. They were not allowed to land in England—although Regardie had been born there—but had to await Crowley in Brussels. Crowley himself left France in a blaze of publicity in the following month; since his expulsion from Sicily, he had been a subject of intense interest to the world's press. He managed to secure a British passport for Maria by the simple expedient of marrying her. Then he and Regardie were able to resume their work, this time at Knockholt, in Kent. Regardie records that when Gerald Yorke came to visit, Crowley would play them both simultaneouly at blindfold chess, sitting with his back to them in an armchair, and calling out the moves; he would always beat them both. The story reveals how much skill in 'visualization' Crowley had achieved through his studies of magic.

Crowley had now completed what many regard as his major work, *Magick in Theory and Practice*, basically a sequel to the earlier *Book Four*. Gerald Yorke and Karl Germer paid for its publication in Paris—no English publisher would touch it, perhaps because Crowley recommended sacrificing a male child to achieve the best magical results, and added a footnote to the effect that he himself had done so about a hundred and fifty times a year between 1912 and 1928. And even in this, his major work, Crowley was unable to resist the temptation to indulge in sadistic practical joking; a practising magician explained to the present writer that the book was 'booby trapped'—that is, that certain 'deliberate mistakes' have been included in its magic rituals. To the non-occultist this may sound harmless enough. But it is a basic part of the magical tradition that demonic entities are sticklers for precision and accuracy, and that the smallest slip can bring disaster. Crowley obviously liked the idea of some neophyte magician pronouncing magic spells in a graveyard by moonlight, and being possessed by some sinister entity from 'beyond the threshold'.

It is a measure of Crowley's total lack of realism that he believed that *Magick* would finally establish his reputation with the general public (he explains that he has written it 'to help the banker, the pugilist. . . the grocer, the factory girl. . .' etc.). In fact, it was not even noticed by reviewers.

Things looked slightly more promising for the 'auto-hagiography.' He discovered a small press in Museum Street, Mandrake Press, run by Edward Goldston. Collins had, of course, lost interest in the book after the *Sunday Express* attacks; in June 1929, Crowley signed a contract with Mandrake Press, with an advance of £50. Goldston's partner, an Australian named P. R. Stephenson, was a great admirer of Crowley, and was engaged in writing a defense of the much-maligned magician—although this was not so much a labour of love as a business precaution, designed to break down sales resistance to Crowley's *Confessions* and to his witchcraft novel *Moonchild* (written in New Orleans in 1917). Regrettably, Crowley's reputation was so unsavoury that none of these books made any impact. *Moonchild* appeared later in 1929, accompanied by a note that begins:

> This entrancing story, by one of the most mysterious and brilliant of living writers, describes the magickal operation by which a spirit of the moon was invoked into the being of an expectant mother despite the machinations of the Black Lodge of rival magicians. . . [And it ends, significantly]: Aleister Crowley's first novel, *The Diary of a Drug Fiend*, was withdrawn from circulation after an attack in the sensational press.

It is utterly typical of Crowley that when, in 1933, he saw a copy of *Moonchild* in a bookshop in Praed Street, with a card that stated: 'Aleister Crowley's first novel *The Diary of a Drug Fiend* was withdrawn from circulation after an attack in the sensational press', he instantly sued the bookshop for libel, pointing out that the book had simply gone out of print, and won £50 damages with costs. It seems a pity that the bookshop owner (a Mr Gray) did not have the presence of mind to point out to the judge that he was quoting Crowley's own words from the blurb of *Moonchild*.

When the first two volumes of the *Confessions* appeared in 1930 (it was designed to be published in six) the Mandrake salesman tried in vain to persuade bookshops to offer it for sale. The man who had committed 'unutterable obscenities' at his abbey in Sicily was too hot to handle. As far as the British public was concerned, he should have been in prison, not openly trying to peddle his disgusting life story. The cover design, with its 'idealized self-portrait' and signature whose initial letter was obviously an erect penis, must have put off anyone who thought that 'confessions' implied some kind of repentance.

With regard to the *Confessions* and *Moonchild*, it must be admitted that, for once, Crowley's attitude of injured innocence was justified. The *Confessions* may not be comparable to Cellini, as Cammell suggests, but it is a fascinating book, and not even remotely obscene. *Moonchild* is a highly readable novel; two or three decades later, it might have achieved a success like that of *The Exorcist* or *Rosemary's Baby*. The other small book published by Mandrake—*The Stratagem and Other Stories*—reads at times like a mixture of Borges and Lovecraft, and confirms that Crowley was a born writer. These books were ignored simply because Crowley was Crowley—the 'wickedest man in the world.' And while his reputation was certainly his own fault, it seems a pity that their very real merits were ignored. In any case, Crowley soon quarrelled with Gerald Yorke and Karl Germer—though in neither case was the break a permanent one—and Mandrake Press ceased to exist.

Early in 1930, Crowley was asked to lecture at the Poetry Society at Oxford, and proposed to talk about Gilles de Rais, the fifteenth century child murderer, whom Crowley rightly described as a practitioner of black magic; the authorities banned the lecture, and Crowley countered by having it printed as a pamphlet. When he tried to arrange an exhibition of his paintings, London art galleries declined the honour; when he proposed to show them at another address, where he was negotiating for the lease of a flat, the agent cancelled the lease. Soon after this, he abandoned his wife Maria, went off to Berlin, and found himself a nineteen year old mistress named Hanni Jaegar, whom he called the Monster. Later that year he went off to Spain with Hanni, and performed some spectacular operations of sexual magic with her; but she grew sick of magic, and after a violent quarrel, they were ordered to leave their hotel. After this, Hanni left him and fled back to Germany. Crowley decided to 'annoy' her by pretending to commit suicide; so at a steep cliff called Hell's Mouth, near Cintra, he left a suicide note under his cigarette case. Then he hastened off in pursuit of Hanni. Impressed by his devotion, she again gave herself to him in Berlin. While the world press speculated about his suicide, Crowley persuaded her to lodge a formal complaint—implying sexual harassment— against an American consul who had befriended her in Lisbon and advised her to go home. He was (as Regardie had observed) a man who could nurse a grudge for a long time. The speculation about him ceased when he appeared at the opening of an exhibition of his paintings in Berlin. But this piece of pointless exhibitionism only deepened the general impression that he was a man who would do anything for self-advertisement.

In England, his wife Maria had become an alcoholic, then went insane and had to be committed to Colney Hatch asylum. Crowley's plans to divorce her and marry Hanni Jaegar were shelved when he met another Scarlet Woman named Billy Busch; Symonds' account makes it clear that his relationship with her was as tempestuous as the one with Leah had been. Gerald Hamilton—Christopher Isherwood's 'Mr Norris'—came back to the flat he was sharing with them one day to find her drugged and tied up with ropes, while a note from Crowley ordered him not to release her on any account.

It was in May, 1933, that Crowley—as already mentioned— had sued a Praed Street bookseller for advertising *Moonchild* with a note stating that Crowley's previous novel had been withdrawn from circulation. When the judge awarded Crowley £50, his taste for litigation was whetted. Earlier in life he had wisely steered clear of lawyers; now in perpetual need of money, he bitterly regretted not suing Beaverbrook for the *Sunday Express* 'libels.' So when he came upon a passage in the autobiography of his old Soho friend Nina Hamnett, mentioning that he was accused of practising black magic, Crowley saw another opportunity to raise the wind. He approached her and explained that they could both benefit financially if he won a case against her publisher, Constable and Co (of whom Bernard Shaw was a main shareholder). How far she agreed to participate in this unpleasant charade is not clear. At all events, Crowley began to look around for friends to support him in court. J. W. N. Sullivan declined; so did Captain [now Major General] Fuller; so did the novelist J. D. Beresford, who had recommended *Drug Fiend* for publication.

Memories of the law case of 1910 should have warned Crowley that he was tempting the fates. Even without the reputation of the wickedest man in the world, he could not have expected heavy damages for the statement that 'he was supposed to have practised Black Magic' in Cefalu. As it was, his decision to sue Nina Hamnett was as rash as Wilde's decision to sue the Marquis of Queensberry for implying he was a homosexual.

When the trial opened, on 10 April 1934, Crowley soon made a bad impression with his flippancy. Asked whether 'Master Therion'—'the Great Wild Beast'—was a fair expression of his outlook on life, Crowley replied that it meant sunlight, and that they could call him Little Sunshine. He denied that he had been defying all moral conventions since his youth—a statement that may have been expedient but was certainly a lie, and a denial of all his basic principles. Readings from Crowley's erotic poetry shocked the court just as much as the prosecuting counsel knew they would, and even Crowley's comment: 'As *you* read it, it is magnificent' failed to lighten the atmosphere. When Betty May gave evidence about the death of her husband, Crowley's last hope of winning the case evaporated. (He had taken the precaution of having some of her letters stolen from her, but they did him no good in court.) Finally, the judge could contain himself no longer; he interupted to say that in forty years in the legal profession, he thought he had seen every form of wickedness, but now realized he could always learn something new. 'I have never heard such dreadful, horrible, blasphemous and abominable stuff as that which has been produced by the man who describes himself to you as the greatest living poet.' When he asked the jury if they wanted the case to go on, they lost no time in returning a verdict against Crowley.

John Symonds makes the interesting observation that in spite of his defeat, Crowley felt elated. 'The newspaper sellers had shouted out his name in the streets of London and elsewhere. The world had stopped and stared and wondered.' Nothing could reveal more plainly that strange lack of realism that prevented Crowley from getting to grips with the world of actuality. The truth is that all Crowley's hopes, all his ambitions, had collapsed when Betty May and Mary Butts denounced him in the *Sunday Express*. He had always wanted to be recognized as a great poet, as a prophet, as a messiah; after the *Sunday Express* revelations, he had no more chance of achieving these ambitions than of becoming Archbishop of Canterbury. Yet his understanding of his own situation was so poor that he felt that being called horrible, blasphemous and abominable was a step in the direction of the recognition he craved. Perhaps it was just as well. Some men are improved by facing total failure and learning to draw on their inner resources; but Crowley had never been of this type. Self-discipline could only carry him so far; then he had to turn for support to drugs, women and disciples. An accurate assessment of his situation in 1934 would probably have destroyed him.

As it was, the gods sent him immediate solace. As he left the court, a nineteen-year-old girl rushed up to him, and told him she thought the verdict was 'the wickedest thing since the crucifixion.' She went on to explain that she would like to become the mother of his child. This was just what Crowley needed. He rushed her off to his bed, and forgot the defeat in acts of sex magic. Yet his diary for that day reveals a total inability to grasp what had happened: he wrote 'Case violated by Swift [the judge] and Nina. General joy—the consternation of Constable and Co.'—which seems to indicate a state of self-delusion not far from insanity.

Later that year, he again appeared in court, this time to answer the charge of being in possession of Betty May's stolen letters. The man who was responsible for persuading Betty May to bring the case was a friend of Raoul Loveday's called Charles May who, according to Symonds, had also been responsible for having Crowley expelled from Cefalu. He told Symonds: 'I am not at all ashamed of my share in this "Persecution."' Crowley was bound over and ordered to pay fifty guineas costs.

Crowley was to live on for another thirteen years, and yet

there is a sense in which the Nina Hamnett law case marked the end of his career as a magician. There are no more major events in Crowley's life to record, and no more major works to discuss—although many regard his work on the tarot—*The Book of Thoth* (1944)—as a classic in its field.

Crowley was bankrupted by the Hamnett case (although this was less serious than it sounds, since he had no assets anyway). Friends like Germer continued to send him remittances, but certainly not enough to live in the style to which he was accustomed. The actor Oliver Wilkinson, son of Crowley's old friend Louis (Marlow) Wilkinson, mentions that there was a period in the 1930s when Crowley was forced to live in slum lodgings in Paddington Green, and that Louis Wilkinson asked his son not to give Crowley his address if he happened to run into him—when Crowley was broke, he was in the habit of sending frantic telegrams to his friends, some of whom ran themselves deeply into debt to respond to his appeals. But Oliver Wilkinson adds that Crowley soon had money to turn his back on Paddington and return to Piccadilly and Jermyn Street. This may have been due to the sale of Crowley's Elixir of Life pills, which cost twenty-five guineas for enough to last a week, and which were supposed to restore sexual potency and generally increase vitality; his satisfied customers were unaware that the chief ingredient in these pills was Crowley's own sperm. Or it may have been as a result of remittances from a new OTO Lodge in Pasadena, California, the Agape Lodge, which was part of the Church of Thelema. Founded by a Crowley disciple named Wilfred Smith, whom Crowley had met through his 'magical son' Jones in 1915, it was soon taken over by a rocket engineer called Jack Parsons, who later became closely associated with another aspiring young magician named L. Ron Hubbard, later the founder of Scientology, who soon stole Parson's wife. Hubbard was later to claim that he was actually trying to break up this 'evil black magic group', and that he actually succeeded; but the letters Parsons wrote to Crowley in the 1940s—which are quoted in *The Great Beast*—leave no doubt that Parsons regarded Hubbard as a genuine magical neophyte. Parsons later blew himself up in an experiment with rocket fuel. Oliver Wilkinson mentions that when he knew Crowley in the 1940s, Crowley's rent was paid by the Pasadena sect.

Oliver Wilkinson also leaves no doubt that Crowley's influence could be highly destructive. His father and mother met Crowley in New York towards the end of the First World War; his mother, Frances, was an American poetess. (Louis Wilkinson, who was, at that time, a well known man of letters, is now remembered mainly as a friend of the Powys brothers.) Frances took an instant dislike to Crowley from the first time they went to have dinner with him in his skyscraper apartment in New York. Wilkinson, who was normally a self-controlled man, behaved extravagantly and foolishly at dinner, and Frances seems to have suspected that Crowley was exercising some kind of sinister hypnotic influence over him. Later, Crowley turned Wilkinson so thoroughly against her that he persuaded him to have her certified insane; Frances got wind of the plot and succeeded in escaping. But when she returned home later, in a state of physical weakness and psychological shock, she found Crowley at the top of the stair, holding her three year old son Oliver by the hand. Crowley murmured:

> I met a silly woman yesterday... She had not approved of my friendship with her husband... She returned home to find her two lovely babes on the mat in front of the fire in extraordinary positions [she said] without their heads. This woman could *imagine* her babies' heads rolling on the carpet—rolling!... cut off in their infancy. Poor mad woman—she imagined *I* had done it.

This was clearly an attempt by Crowley to drive Frances Wilkinson mad by a form of hypnotic suggestion. It did not work; Frances managed to persuade one of the doctors—who was supposed to certify her—to tell her about Crowley's libellous allegations. Crowley was sufficiently alarmed—perhaps at the thought of another court case—to drop his threats. He apparently ceased to visit the Wilkinsons because he knew that Frances was aware he wore a wig (for some reason, he flatly denied this) and was awaiting a chance to tear it off. (Many commentators have remarked on Crowley's immense vanity.) But he warned her that he would follow her wherever she went. Later, after she and Louis Wilkinson had divorced, she found 'tramp's signs' outside the gate of her cottage in Essex, and recognised them as Crowley's magical symbols. Oliver Wilkinson comments: 'None of us ever felt before or since such intensity of terror as then descended on us.' It is an interesting example of that odd malevolence, the tendency to nurse grudges, that prevented Crowley achieving the kind of greatness he used to dream about. He remained essentially a petty human being.

Like so many of Crowley's 'Scarlet Women', the nineteen-year-old girl who had approached him after the Nina Hamnett trial ended up in a mental home. Dorothy Olsen, the American woman who had stolen Crowley from Leah, drank herself to death. Hanni Jaegar, the German girl with whom he had gone to Spain, committed suicide soon after their separation. Symonds quotes Kenneth Grant to the effect that Crowley chose these borderline women because of 'their aptitude for getting on the Astral Plane more easily than the average, better integrated person.' But it is difficult not to feel that Crowley went through life trailing some cloak of death and insanity behind him.

Crowley remained in London throughout the war, at 93 Jermyn Street, until, in 1944, he moved down to Aston Clinton, in Buckinghamshire, where he lodged at the Bell Inn. It was the flying bombs that led to the move. He soon found it too lonely, and asked Louis Wilkinson to try and find him somewhere else. Wilkinson asked his son Oliver, and when Oliver mentioned it in the dressing room of the Hastings theatre where he was acting, one of the actors said he was opening an 'intellectual guest house.' On 17 January 1945, Crowley moved into Netherwood, the Ridge, Hastings. Oliver Wilkinson, who had not seen Crowley since he was three, was surprised when he met him again. 'I had expected a pretentious warlock, a dangerous clown, and I found an intelligent man... He was intelligent, with an intelligence that dried the air.' Crowley sent Oliver a box of 'the most expensive cigars in the world.' Unaware until too late of how good they were, Oliver smoked them all, then confessed to Crowley that he had smoked them without appreciating them. Crowley thought he was asking for more, and sent another lot—a typical example of the generosity that was part of Crowley's charm.

This last decade was not entirely unfruitful. In 1939 he delivered in London a series of Eight Lectures on Yoga, which show Crowley at his best—witty, combative, almost Shavian in tone, although the tendency to make schoolboy jokes remains: 'In highly civilized communitites like our own (loud laughter). . .' But its eighty pages reveal that, in spite of the heroin and cocaine, Crowley's intelligence was as dry and sharp as ever.

In 1943, Crowley met a woman who asked his advice on 'occult, spiritual and practical matters', and Crowley wrote her a series of letters beginning 'Cara Soror'. He was back in his element again—the master giving advice to the disciple. In fact, he so enjoyed writing her letters that he asked other disciples to ask him questions. He intended to publish the result under the title *Aleister Explains Everything*, but never got around to it. The letters (eighty of them) were finally published by Karl Germer, in 1954, as *Magick Without Tears*, and they are probably the best introduction to Crowley's ideas in existence. The tone is casual and light hearted, but he throws in some of his keenest insights: for example, after a letter devoted mainly to debunking astrology, he admits that, for some odd reason, it seems to work, and adds: 'I see no objection at all to postulating that certain "rays" or other means of transmitting some peculiar form or forms of energy, may reach us from other parts of the solar system. . .' What is so remarkable about Crowley the 'magician' is that he remains Crowley the scientist, and always applies the same probing intellectual curiosity to every field he surveys. This is ultimately the most impressive quality about his mind, and the one that might—if he had concentrated on developing it to the full—have brought him the fame he craved. Crowley's tragedy was that he never concentrated for long enough to develop anything to the full.

The other major impression to emerge from *Magick Without Tears* is that—as odd as it sounds—one of Crowley's chief drawbacks was his sense of humour. This is a disability he shares with Bernard Shaw: both were driven by a strange compulsion to be flippant. But when he becomes absorbed in ideas, Shaw can remain serious for a sufficiently long time to convince the reader of his intellectual stature. In Crowley, the flippancy has the tone of a schoolmaster trying to be funny for the benefit of the sixth form, or a muscular Christian trying to convince you that he isn't really religious. 'How can a yogi ever be worried?. . . *That* question I have been expecting for a

very long time!' (Crowley has never learned that exclamation
marks give the impression of a gushing schoolgirl.) 'And
what *you* expect is to see my middle stump break the wicket-
keeper's nose, with the balls smartly fielded by Third Man
and Short Leg!' It makes us aware that there was something
wrong with Crowley's 'self image.' He is one of those people
who, no matter how hard they try, never feel quite grown up.

The best description of Crowley in this late period can be
found in *The Magick of Aleister Crowley* by John Symonds.[1] In
the early 1940s, Symonds moved into a flat at 84 Boundary
Road, Hampstead, where Victor Neuburg had died in 1940.
He became curious about the man who had 'cursed' Neuburg,
and sent Crowley a telegram asking him if he would write an
article on magic for a literary magazine. Crowley asked him
down to Hastings for lunch. Symonds was accompanied by
the astrologer Rupert Gleadow. 'Netherwood' was in a
country lane, and stood in private grounds. As they stood
waiting, a slow, feeble step sounded on the stairs, and an old
man in plus fours, with a goatee beard and a bald head,
intoned querulously: 'Do what thou wilt shall be the whole of
the law.' When Gleadow was introduced as an astrologer,
Crowley remarked that he thought there was less than one
per cent truth in astrology. Crowley had an odd stare; his eyes
were 'unusually wide as if he were prepared to hypnotise us.'
'I began to feel that there was something a little strange about
Crowley. It was difficult to say what, exactly, it was. Apart
form the ring and the brooch, and his peculiar sweetish smell
(due to the holy oil of Abra-Melin the Mage) he might be
considered, I thought, an ordinary old man; and yet there was
a quality of remoteness about him. . . I can best describe this
quality by saying that it suggested that he cared very little for
the usual occupations and considerations of mankind. He
had, however, one common failing: he was ambitious, and
did not want to depart hence without leaving as great a mark
upon the earth as possible.'

After lunch they drank brandy and Crowley talked about
prophecies of the end of the world, a matter in which he was
evidently well versed. He mentioned Nostradamus's prediction

1. Much of this was incorporated into the revised edition of *The
Great Beast*, but the earlier book deserves to be read for its own sake.

that Doomsday would occur in 1999, but was evidently unimpressed by it. So this thin, dessicated old man, whose daily doses of heroin would kill a normal man, was the formidable Great Beast, now old, bored and rather pathetic. His subsequent correspondence with Symonds occasionally has a querulous tone, as if he felt he was being neglected, and he sometimes signed his letters 'Aleister.' (In earlier days, acquaintances had always addressed him as Crowley, or A.C, or Beast.) Symonds often had to hold him steady as he injected himself in the armpit. And Symonds was responsible for the publication of Crowley's final volume of verse, *Olla*— which, as usual, was almost totally ignored by reviewers.

The juvenile sense of humour remained in evidence. He told Symonds of a visit from a military man, who had pulled such a face when Crowley prepared to inject himself that Crowley went into the bathroom. There he placed his mouth near the keyhole and proceeded to squeal like a stuck pig. When he came out, the military man looked sick and shaken.

Symonds saw the news of his death on the front pages of the newspapers, together with photographs of the 'wickedest man in the world.' Crowley would have been flattered. He had died of myocardial degeneration and chronic bronchitis on the night of 1 December, 1947. On Friday 5 December, Crowley was cremated at Brighton. Various ex-disciples and ex-mistresses were present, as well as Symonds and Gerald Yorke. Louis Wilkinson then read aloud Crowley's *Hymn to Pan*, beginning:

> Thrill with lissome lust of the light,
> O man! My Man!
> Come careering out of the night
> Of Pan! Io Pan!

Crowley had also requested that the whole *Book of the Law* should be read aloud but—perhaps because this would have taken at least an hour—Wilkinson read only short extracts. The Brighton Council was shocked to hear what had gone on in their chapel, and a spokesman announced they would take steps to make sure it never occurred again. Since there was only one Aleister Crowley, this was a fairly safe promise to make.

Epilogue

WHEN John Symonds first took his wife Margaret to meet Crowley, she received a powerful impression of evil. 'Yes, evil haunted that face, but the years had diluted its strength.' And after Crowley had talked to her at some length about his trek across China, she felt that the room had become small and oppressive, 'and he flooded me again with a sense of evil, so that I visibly shivered.' But was Crowley really 'evil' or was this largely her imagination? If evil is defined as a pleasure in cruelty or destruction, then Crowley most certainly fails to qualify. He was self-centred, and he did a great number of 'caddish' things; but his worst behaviour was usually like that of a spoilt child.

The argument that Crowley was evil depends upon some of his nastier writings. Oliver Wilkinson mentions that among Crowley's papers, there is a description of tying a negro to a tree, cutting a hole in his stomach, then inserting his penis. If Crowley had ever done such a thing, it would certainly qualify him as genuinely evil. But it is fairly certain that he was not, in the pathological sense, a sadist. The early *Snowdrops from a Curate's Garden* is an attempt to rival Sade. But the very fact that Crowley never returned to sadistic fantasy indicates that it was merely another experiment in shocking the bourgeoisie. It is worth bearing in mind that even Sade himself, who spent his whole life toying with such fantasies, never actually practised them; on one occasion when he had a chance to revenge himself on the mother-in-law who had caused him to be imprisoned for years, he showed Chrisitan forbearance.

The chief impression left by a study of Crowley's life and works is that he wasted an immense amount of time and energy trying to shock everyone he came into contact with, and that his dislike of orthodoxy turned him into an unconsciously comic figure, like Don Quixote. Everyone has experienced a feeling of blind rage against authority—if only when a traffic warden hands them a ticket. And we have all known people in whom some early clash with authority has created a lifelong neurosis, a conditioned reflex of hatred against some group of people—homosexuals, Jews, blacks, policemen... Such people strike us as stupid as well as rather dangerous, because they have become victims of a purely mechanical reaction. Crowley's early contact with religious bigots made him the lifelong victim of such a reaction; the lightest touch on his anti-authority button made him swing into action like a mechanical toy.

The chief problem of this reflex is that it is self-perpetuating. It arouses violent hostility, and the hostility reinforces the original resentment. Caught in this vicious circle, many 'rebels' turn into criminals, and a percentage of such criminals into mass murderers. (The annals of modern crime contain dozens of such cases—Manson, the Moors murderers, the Yorkshire Ripper...) The outraged ego, shaking its fist at authority, becomes trapped in its own resentment until it becomes—in theory at least—capable of destroying all mankind. Sensible people draw back long before they reach this point, and Crowley was restrained by an instinct of self-preservation. But it was this 'criminal' element in him that was sensed by people who felt he was evil.

It is interesting to note Crowley's habit of relieving his bowels on people's carpets. In the twentieth century, this has become an increasingly frequent feature of burglaries, and criminologists recognize it as a gesture of rebellion. The burglar is not merely in someone's apartment for the practical purpose of taking money, but to commit a kind of symbolic rape, to express the resentment of the have-not for the haves. Crowley was expressing a different kind of resentment, but it undoubtedly has the same 'criminal' origin. It has become generally recognized—so much so that it has become a boring commonplace—that this type of pathology is usually associated with a lack of love in childhood. Animal ethologists have observed that creatures who have received no love in the early, formative period of their lives become permanently incapable of feeling affection. Crowley's parents, with their narrow religious obsession, seem to have been the type who were incapable of expressing spontaneous affection. In turn, he became incapable of showing affection for wives or children. Although he occasionally declares in the magical journals that he has 'fallen in love', none of his relationships with women involved what would normally be described as love. Women aroused in him a crude desire to assert his masculinity by penetrating them, which brought a triumphant sense of violation. He wanted them to behave like nymphomaniacs. He wrote of one mistress: 'we went crazy... we tore off our clothes and fucked and fucked and fucked. And suddenly she got a jealous fit about three cheap whores... and I strangled her... Woke up early and finished the fuck.' His relations with women were devoid of the normal element of solicitude or protectiveness.

Sex is certainly the main key to Crowley's mentality; but so is the fact that he was a late Victorian. (The early Victorians were far less prudish than their children; nude mixed bathing was common until the 1860s at seaside resorts.) The Victorians became so embarrassed about sex that they covered up table legs, and invented a special kind of straitjacket for babies to prevent them from touching their genitals in bed. So for Crowley, sex was always something deliciously 'dirty' and wicked. In many ways, his development parallels that of Freud. When, in the 1880s, Freud first began to suspect that sexual frustration might be the key to mental illness, the idea so frightened and shocked him that he hardly dared to put it into words; he felt that it would mean professional disgrace and ruin. And the very fact that the idea created such inner turmoil convinced him that it must be true. If he had lived in a less prudish society, he might simply have concluded that sexual problems can lead to neuroses, and left it at that. But the fact that the idea struck him as too awful to utter led him to go much further, and to assert that *all* neurosis, without exception, has a sexual origin, and to exaggerate the sexual element out of all proportion. Crowley reacted in exactly the same manner. The idea of prostitution, of seduction, of adultery, aroused in him a kind of feverish, panting excitement, and he was quick to suspect anyone with a touch of puritanism of the same violent response. 'I cannot omit to mention one atrocity at Agra. Some prurient English curator had indulged his foul instincts by whitewashing a magnificent fresco in the palace because it was "improper". In other words, he was so leprously lascivious that anything which reminded him of reproduction produced a frenzied spasm of sensuality in his soul...' In fact, the unfortunate curator was probably thinking of the officers' wives and daughters who would be shown around the palace, and trying to spare their blushes. So Crowley's overreaction to authority was compounded with an equally unrealistic overreaction to sex, which led him to believe he was being iconoclastic when he was only sticking out his tongue at long-dead Victorians. His sexual rebellion, like his social rebellion, tends to strike us as much ado about nothing.

It might seem that, for a man handicapped by these paranoid obsessions, chances of real personal development were minimal. But there was a third component in Crowley's peculiar make-up: a kind of romantic mysticism, a feeling that Yeats expressed in the lines:

> ... what the world's million lips are searching for
> Must be substantial somewhere
> and a consequent longing for the 'horns of elfland'.

This is why Eckartshausen's *Cloud Upon the Sanctuary* exercised upon Crowley as powerful an influence as Sinnett's *Esoteric Buddhism* (with its talk of 'Secret Masters') had upon Yeats. Unfortunately, the mystical order described in Eckart-hausen was non-existent. But a chance meeting with George Cecil Jones led Crowley into what seemed to be the next best thing, the Golden Dawn, and established his course for the rest of his life.

This is admittedly the point at which the modern reader tends to lose touch with Crowley and his motivations. The idea of dressing up in ceremonial robes and marching around in circles chanting 'Adonai ha-Aretz, Malkuth, Geburah, Gedulah' sounds rather absurd. Magic seems to be pure self-delusion. But, as I have suggested in the opening chapter, such a view may be superficial. For some strange reason, magic *can* work. And this, as Crowley recognized, is because it is based on a recognition of unknown powers of the human mind. For most of us, the word 'magician' conjures up a picture of a Walt Disney character in a conical hat waving a magic wand. Yet the things that take place at 'spiritualist seances' every day are a kind of magic, and would have been recognized as such by our ancestors. So is the kind of telepathy that takes place between most married couples. So is one of the most commonplace forms of paranormal phenomena known as the 'projection of the double'. In 1881, a student named S. H. Beard told his girlfriend, Miss Verity, that he was going to try to 'appear' to her later that evening, and in due course, Miss Verity and her sister were terrified to see Beard standing in their bedroom, then vanishing into thin air. Beard said he did it by a peculiar 'effort of volition' which he could not describe. The Society for Psychical Research recorded hundreds of such cases in its early days. This is one of the simplest and most straightforward forms of 'magic.'[1]

This is obviously the major question raised by the study of Crowley's life and works. Did he possess magical powers? If so, what were their nature? In the early days, when Crowley was performing magic in his 'temple' in London or at Boleskine House, it seems fairly clear that what he was doing was closely related to what happens in the seance room, (although Crowley always professed a great contempt for seances). And the same is probably true of the strange events described in 'The Visions and the Voice.' But this was not the kind of magic in which Crowley was really interested. Crowley wanted to be a magician because he wanted power— power over other people. (One of his female admirers, Martha Kuntzel, was quite right to see a close resemblance between Crowley and Hitler.) And it seems clear that, in this department, he succeeded. Seabrook's story—related in the first chapter—of how Crowley walked down Fifth Avenue behind a businessman, and caused him to stumble and fall, is a typical example. So is a story related by Oliver Wilkinson, of a house party that took place after the Second World War, when Crowley was 'old and harmless.' Crowley was sitting on his haunches by the fire as two other men talked. One man suddenly fell sideways, his head close to the floor, and stayed there. The other dropped on all fours and began to behave like a dog, barking, whining, scratching the door. Then the

1. For a fuller discussion of such cases, see my *Mysteries*, Part 2, Chapter 7.

other man got up and rushed out of the French windows; he returned the next day, his clothes torn and his face bleeding. Oliver's mother Frances had seen Crowley do something similar in New York—caused a man to act like a dog; when the man recovered, he tried to pass it off as a joke. Frances Wilkinson obviously suspected Crowley of exercising a similar influence on her husband that first evening when they went to dine with Crowley, and Louis Wilkinson began to talk 'extravagantly, in a manner quite unlike his usual self.'

Oliver Wilkinson suggests that Crowley may have achieved these effects by drugs or hypnosis. Neither seems likely, unless we are willing to recognize that there is another form of hypnosis that operates directly from will to will. I have cited elsewhere[2] a number of cases in which hypnotists were apparently able to achieve power over someone by a form of telepathic hypnosis. In the celebrated Heidelberg case, a criminal was able to achieve total power over a woman— even to the point of persuading her to murder her husband— by merely touching her hand. Crowley seems to have had a similar power over certain women. John Symonds tells a story of a titled lady who was looking into the window of Fortnum and Mason when she felt an ominous presence beside her. In the window, she saw Crowley's reflection staring at her. Crowley introduced himself; they vanished into the Ritz [where she was staying] and emerged ten days later. Soon after, her marriage collapsed.[3] Crowley obviously sensed this same susceptibility to his power when he first met Leah Hirsig, and immediately began to kiss her. Leah was not, in fact, Crowley's usual type—he liked well-built, large-breasted women, and Leah was thin and flat chested. But Crowley sensed that she could be entirely dominated by his will. In A Voyage to Arcturus, David Lindsay mentions that this kind of domination 'satisfies the hunger of the will exactly as food satisfies the hunger of the body.' Crowley knew all about the hunger of the will.

Another twentieth century 'magician', Gurdjieff, also seemed to know about these strange powers of the will, although he

2. See Mysteries, pp. 486–491, and A Criminal History of Mankind, p. 28 et seq.
3. The Great Beast, footnote p. 292.

never used them as Crowley did, purely for his own satisfaction. Gurdjieff's chief disciple Ouspensky has described how Gurdjieff was able to communicate with him telepathically by causing a voice to speak inside his chest—even when they were in different rooms. Another follower, Fritz Peters, has described how Gurdjieff was able to cause a girl to faint by merely telling the pianist to play a certain musical chord when she was in the room.[4] Gurdjieff also obviously knew some of the basic tricks of 'magic.' According to Rom Landau, he was also able to exercise a direct sexual influence upon women—one woman felt she had been suddenly 'struck through the sexual centre', and turned to find Gurdjieff's hypnotic gaze fixed upon her. Gurdjieff and Crowley seem to have met only once, when Crowley went to tea at Gurdjieff's priory at Fontainebleau; Gurdjieff apparently kept a watchful eye on Crowley, and C. S. Nott said of this meeting: 'I got a strong impression of two magicians, the white and the black—the one strong, powerful, full of light: the other also powerful, but heavy, dull, ignorant.'[5]

This, then, was the kind of magic Crowley knew how to exercise. He also seems to have possessed, to a high degree, the power that Jung called 'active imagination'—the power to descend into the unconscious and see 'visions.' This is—as we have already noted—the power that the Kabbalist quite deliberately sets out to cultivate, and accounts of it can be found in most books on magic.[6] We have seen that Crowley understood one of the basic secrets of the human mind: how to side-step the everyday personality and descend into the deeper levels of the mind; he showed Jane Wolfe how to call upon this power when he forced her to make a 'magical retirement' in a tent near the abbey of Thelema. And Crowley himself learned to call upon these powers of the unconscious mind—or the right brain—in his own magical retirements: for example, in the sixth of his *Eight Lectures on Yoga*, he describes a vision he experienced during a magical retirement

4. See my book *The War Against Sleep*, pp. 32 and 63.
5. See *The Occult*, p. 401.
6. See, for example, Israel Regardie's *Foundations of Practical Magic* (1979) and W. E. Butler's *The Magician, His Training and Work* (1959.)

near Lake Pasquaney in New Hampshire, when he saw a representation of the universe in which he saw that the stars were actually ideas and souls, and that the rays connecting them were—paradoxically—also stars.

All this offers us one of the clearest clues to the nature of magic. Human beings find it very hard to realize that the experience of boredom and futility is an experience of feeling trapped in the external world, and that the experience of freedom consists of a *descent into oneself*. It may seem self evident, for example, that when a man is involved in lovemaking, his consciousness is focused upon the other person. In fact, a little introspection reveals that this is not so. The more deeply he is involved in lovemaking, the more deeply his centre of consciousness is 'inside' himself—just as, for example, when he is listening to music. It is as if he takes the girl (or the music) *inside* himself. The more we feel trapped in the external universe, the more we feel helpless and 'contingent.' The more we can descend 'inside' ourselves, the more we feel a curious certainty that no unexpected catastrophes will occur—and this seems to be borne out by experience.

Jung noted that it is in these 'inward' states in which we experience strange 'synchronicities'—oddly significant co-incidences. When, for example, I am working well, and am absorbed in what I am doing, I often seem to 'stumble' upon exactly the piece of information that I shall need for the next page or so, and I have described elsewhere[7] how, when I was writing an article about synchronicity, absurd synchronicities began to occur in startling profusion, as if to reinforce my conviction that I was on the right track. 'Magic' seems to be, to some extent, inducing these states of mind in which synchronicities will occur. And since we *can* induce these states of mind—albeit rather haphazardly—this means that there is an element of natural magic about everyday living. We are all apprentice magicians.

So we can see that Crowley—in spite of that lifelong element of delinquency—was pursuing the basic 'romantic quest' in his own special way. This is why he could, even in his worst moments, feel a certain self-justification. In spite of his faults, he was engaged in his own rather bumbling, incompetent

7. In *An Encyclopedia of Unsolved Mysteries*.

quest for the absolute. When he wrote poetry, when he climbed mountains, when he practised his magical incantations, he experienced the sudden glow of meaning, of immense affirmation. This is why he never ceased to insist that he was a mystic. This is why, even when he had just indulged in some appallingly selfish piece of behaviour, he could assure himself that he had never betrayed his ideals.

Crowley's problem is summarized in the comment of Mencius—already quoted: 'Those who follow the part of themselves that is great will become great men; those who follow the part of themselves that is small will become small men.' We all consist of many possible selves, and our experience and our behaviour nourishes different aspects of ourselves. Every one of us contains a bit of Saint Francis of Assisi and a bit of Jack the Ripper, as well as assorted fragments of Casanova, John Knox, Einstein, Scrooge, Plato, W. C. Fields and a hundred others. The personality that finally becomes dominant depends partly upon chance, but much more upon individual choice. Acts of free will determine the ultimate balance. Crowley, for all his geniune idealism, leaned heavily towards self-indulgence. So when it became a choice between his own convenience and that of somebody else, he invariably chose himself. Every time the Shelley inside him started to gain the ascendancy, it was outmanoevred by the Flashman.

One of the most puzzling things about Crowley is that he was so lacking in critical insight into himself. He could always manage to find some justification, even for his worst pieces of behaviour. Oddly enough, he possessed a highly developed sense of 'karma' or destiny, the feeling that life is full of hidden meanings, and that our conduct determines our fate. Yet as he left a trail of destruction and betrayals behind him, it never seemed to strike him that this same 'law' would sooner or later involve him in retribution. Reading about Crowley produces the same sensation as reading about Al Capone or Lucky Luciano or Bonnie and Clyde: that his downfall was somehow inevitable. There is a feeling that a man who deserts his wife and child and sacrifices a cat and forces his mistress to submit to intercourse with a goat is somehow creating his own bad luck.

How, then, do we explain the currrent Crowley revival,

which has led to all his major works (and many of the minor ones) being reprinted? This is partly because Crowley symbolizes a kind of mindless rebellion against authority. He has become—as Symonds points out—the 'unsung hero of the hippies'; his 'Do what thou wilt' appeals to the feelings that produced the pot-smoking, flower-power rebellion of the 60s, as well as to the hatred of authority that led Hell's Angels to smear themselves in excrement. If Crowley had been alive in the era of Charles Manson and later of the Sex Pistols, he would have found a host of enthusiastic followers.

But there is also a more discriminating response to Crowley's message. After the Second World War, there was a strong revival of interest in 'occultism.' The law that made witchcraft illegal in England was repealed in 1951, and three years later, a 'witch' called Gerald Gardner published *Witchcraft Today*, alleging that there are still dozens of covens— groups of witches—practising all over England. He explained that they were followers of a nature-religion called wicca. Gardner was a friend of Crowley's, and an initiate of the OTO, and Crowley authorised him to set up his own magical group. Gardner liked being flagellated, and his version of wicca laid heavy emphasis on sex rites in which everyone was nude. Understandably, it quickly gained hordes of disciples. Crowley's version of 'magick' was, naturally, much in evidence in these covens. Many members of such groups lost interest as they got older; others developed a wider interest in magic, and studied seriously the Enochian system of John Dee, the magic of the Golden Dawn, and Crowley's own sex-orientated system. For readers wishing to learn more of the modern magical revival, there are excellent books by writers like Francis King, Stephen Skinner and Robert Turner. These make it clear that there is a strong connection between magic and Jung's concepts of active imagination and synchronicity.

After Crowley's death, Karl Germer became the active head of the OTO, although there continued to be splinter groups, particularly in Germany. (This has greatly confused the question of Crowley copyright, for Crowley left copyright in his works to the OTO, and several groups can therefore claim to own them.) It was Germer who gave a charter to an occultist named Kenneth Grant to set up his own OTO group in England. Germer later regretted his decision, and told

Grant he was expelled, but Grant has continued to regard himself as head of the British organization of the OTO. In this capacity, he has written a number of remarkable and fascinating books on magic, with titles like *The Magical Revival* and *Aleister Crowley and the Hidden God*, the first of which is probably the best history of modern magic in existence. Grant is less interested in Crowley's defects as a human being than in his insights as a magician, and he takes *The Book of the Law* as seriously as Crowley took it himself. Being, in general, a far clearer writer than Crowley, and lacking Crowley's tendency to drag in his own personality, he is a far better exponent of Crowleyan 'magick' than Crowley himself.

Yet in spite of Grant's skilful advocacy, it is difficult to take Crowley seriously, even as a student of magic. The hatred of religion and the conviction that he himself was the new messiah taints all his serious work with a kind of silliness, just as *The Book of the Law* is tainted by his Swinburnian tendency to childish blasphemy. The anti-authoritarianism which originated in his dislike of the Plymouth Brethren led to an emphasis on the pleasures of the senses that strikes us as absurdly exaggerated; all the talk about lissom lusts and scarlet sins seems as old fashioned as the Yellow Book and Wilde's 'love that dare not speak its name.' Again and again, his ideas are marred by a kind of crudity that makes them seem too obvious, so the reader has an impulse to murmur 'Elementary, my dear Crowley.'

This can be seen clearly in his psychological system, as expounded to Frank Bennett at the Abbey of Thelema. The subconscious mind (Freud would have said the unconscious) is our true self, and we should not try to repress its desires. This is where the Plymouth Brethren went wrong—trying to weaken their sexual desires until they had become seething masses of repression. Freedom consists in ceasing to repress the subconscious mind, and instead, learning to do its will. . .

This may be good Freudianism, but it is bad 'occultism.' Traditional occultism has always been based upon the view that man possesses a 'higher will', and that his problem is to learn to act in accordance with it. Aldous Huxley once summarized this view as the notion that the human mind possesses an unconscious basement, full of black beetles and vermin, but that it also possesses a *superconscious attic*, which is as much 'above' ordinary consciousness as the basement is below it. Huxley suggests that it is this 'attic' which is responsible for paranormal powers like telepathy, second sight and precognition.

Crowley's psychological theories were so limited by his anti-authoritarianism and his sexual obsession that such a notion would have been completely beyond him. He often stated that 'Do what thou wilt' did not mean 'Do whatever you like' but 'Do your *true* will.' But this simple Freudian plan of the mind—bungalow-with-basement—meant that, like Freud, he felt that the basic answer lay in freedom from repression—in 'letting it all hang out.' And this is, in fact, what he practised, and encouraged his followers to practise—with results that could be seen in the cigarette-addicted five year old at the Abbey, and in Crowley's own slavery to heroin. Crowley, like Freud, 'sold human nature short', and his ideas—as expressed, for example, in *The Confessions*—seem oddly crude and simplistic, as if there was a whole dimension of meaning that he completely overlooked. The same applies to his poetry, where the use of overcoloured adjectives cannot disguise the lack of genuinely poetic dimension, a sense of 'unknown modes of being'. And since Crowley himself failed to see this, the final impression he leaves behind is that his ultimate defect was lack of judgement.

Yet when all this has been said, it has to be admitted that there is still an element in Crowley that commands respect. In moods of depression, he himself often recognized the defects of his character. Yet he insisted that these were unimportant compared to the doctrines for which he was the chosen vessel. This is why he wanted the complete *Book of the Law* read aloud at his funeral service. He believed he had been the recipient of an important message, and that it was his task to convey it to the rest of the human race. He was being perfectly serious when he compared himself to Mohammed, and he believed that the *Book of the Law* would one day be recognized as the new *Koran*. 'I, the Beast, the Man Aleister Crowley, whose number is 666, help to show forth this truth to men.'

And what precisely is this truth? It can be summarized in four propositions: (1) Do what thou wilt shall be the whole of the law, (2) Love is the law, love under will, (3) Every man and woman is a star, and (4) Magick is the Science and Art of causing Change to occur in conformity with the Will. The first two propositions are not, in fact, to be found in *The Book of the Law*; they are Crowley's own formulation of its central message. The fourth proposition (from *Magick in Theory and Practice*) is Crowley's central definition of magic. The *Book of the Law* states: 'The word of the law is *thelema*.' On this, Crowley commented: 'Compare Rabelais. Also it may be translated, "Let Will and Action be in harmony." He then adds: 'But *thelema* also means Will in the higher sense of Magical One-pointedness, and in the sense used by Schopenhauer and Fichte.' But we can cut through all the confusions about its meaning if we simply recognize that Crowley had spent his childhood listening to statements about 'the will of God.' His parents were the kind of people who would preface any statement of intention with 'God willing' or 'If it be the will of God.' The state of mind induced by such a continual affirmation is that the universe is, for all practical purposes, predetermined, and that man possesses no free will.

It is interesting to note that when Crowley began to study magic and mysticism, he still found himself haunted by the Christian God; the name can be found on every page of *The Cloud Upon the Sanctuary*, as well as in the *Book of Abra-Melin the Mage* and in the rituals of the Golden Dawn. Crowley must have felt he had escaped one insidious form of Christianity only to fall victim to another. A testimony to his exasperation can be found on the title page of one of his earliest works, *The High History of Good Sir Palomedes*, where the date is given as 'Anno Pseudo Christi MCMXII'. Crowley could not feel free until he had created his own religion *without* the Christian God or its 'pseudo saviour.'

Once we can grasp that *acceptance of human free will* is the core of Crowley's religion, then it can be seen that 'Do what thou wilt' is more than a restatement of Rabelais's motto; it represents a major philosophical affirmation. That he thought of it in this way is clear from his mention of Schopenhauer and Fichte. In Schopenhauer, the Will is the truth behind the world of illusions and appearances. And the most important recognition of the philosopher Fichte is that as soon as man launches himself into action, he becomes conscious of his freedom—a freedom that eludes him while he contents himself with mere thinking. One of Rudolf Steiner's earliest and most important books was called *The Philosophy of Freedom*, and was an attack on scientific materialism and an assertion of the reality of the human will. If Crowley had started his career with a similar book, it would be a great deal easier to understand his significance as a thinker. The discovery that man possesses a 'controlling ego', which presides *over* consciousness, is the foundation stone of his magical philosophy. This is why, while agreeing that 'love is the law', he insists: 'Love *under will*'. According to Christianity, love is the essence of the created universe; God is love, and the basic teaching of Christianity is that men should love one another. Crowley agrees, but he cannot accept that love is the be-all and end-all of the universe: so he adds the all-important postscript: 'Love under will'. Free will is the foundation stone, not love.

When man stops thinking of himself as a mere passive 'creature', and grasps that he is free, he at last ceases to be a mediocrity; he grasps that he is, in fact, a 'star'. In 1922, Crowley told Sullivan:

Every man and woman is a star. You, being a man, are therefore a star. The soul of a star is what we call genius. You are a genius. This fact is obscured either by moral complexes which enmesh it, or lack of adequate machinery to express it...

Sullivan took Crowley's words to heart, wrote his perplexities and frustrations out of his system in an excellent autobiography, then went on to become the first rate writer that Crowley knew him to be. He is a good advertisement for Crowley's conviction that every man and woman is a star.

But perhaps the most interesting of all the propositions that Crowley deduced from his recognition of free will was his belief that magic is the science and art of causing changes to occur in conformity with the will. Other modern thinkers have asserted that the essence of human existence is freedom—notably the 'existentialists'. But most of them feel that, although man is free, he is trapped in a world of matter which always has the last word. Man is free, but his freedom is purely a mental attribute, the 'eternal spirit of the chainless mind.' It cannot save him from suffering and dying miserably. Crowley's deepest instincts revolted against this poor-spirited view. He was convinced that, once a man has *grasped* his own freedom, he ceases to be the helpless victim of circumstance; he can somehow cause changes to occur in conformity with his will. Man's mind has exactly the same power as his hands: not merely to grasp the world, but to *change* it.

But if the man is free, what can he *do* with his freedom? How can he express it? Crowley's first solution to this problem was to travel round the world and sail up crocodile-infested rivers and climb mountains: in short, to become an adventurer. This failed because, as Chesterton rightly observes, an adventure is only an inconvenience rightly considered, and inconvenience is not particularly uplifting to the soul. Crowley's next venture was to award himself various honorary titles, publish books at his own expense, and try to become a celebrity. This was also a failure, largely due to lack of public interest. Finally as a last resort, Crowley returned to magic— and instantly achieved remarkable success. Crowley discovered, to his astonishment, that the Enochian 'calls' really worked. And when Reuss initiated him into the secrets of sexual magic, he felt he had finally solved the problem of expressing his 'true will'. *The Book of the Law* says: 'Take your fill and will of love as ye will, when, where and with whom ye will! But always unto me.' That is, have as much sex as you like, but dedicate each sexual act to the Holy Guardian Angel. Crowley carried out these instructions to the letter, and apparently achieved magical visions, like the one at Lake Pasquaney. Convinced that he was at last on the right track, he devoted the rest of his life to the study of magic and *The Book of the Law*. And disciples like Bennett, Loveday, Mudd, Regardie and Cammell became convinced that Crowley's claim to be the founder of the new religion was factually true. They grasped that the essence of this new religion was human free will, and recognized that, in this basic respect, it differed fundamentally from Buddhism, Judaism, Christianity, Islam and the rest.

There was, however, another basic difference between these earlier religions and the faith of thelema. They had been founded by avatars or prophets who identified themselves totally with their teachings. Crowley admitted freely that he had done his best to evade his responsibility as the custodian of *The Book of the Law*. Disciples like Norman Mudd and Leah Hirsig recognized this when they denounced Crowley for ceasing to be faithful to *The Book of the Law*, and declared themselves the new custodians. The religion of thelema claimed to be the direct word of some superhuman entity, who announced the coming of the new age, and its basic teaching was the reality of free will. Crowley regarded himself as an extremely imperfect mouthpiece of this teaching. But he also believed that any final merit he possessed was the result of having been chosen to propagate the religion of Ra-Hoor-Khuit.

The priest of Ra-Hoor-Khuit was a failure as a human being, as he himself was inclined to acknowledge in moments of honesty. But he thought that unimportant compared to the religion of thelema, the philosophy of human free will that would enable man to evolve to a higher stage. If we ignore Crowley and concentrate on the philosophy, it seems highly probable that he was right.

Bibliography

Cammell, Charles Richard, *Aleister Crowley, The Man: The Mage: The Poet* (University Books, 1962).

Crowley, Aleister:
The Tale of Archais (Kegan Paul, Trench, Trubner & Co., 1898).
Ambergris: A Selection from the Poems of Aleister Crowley (Elkin Mathews, 1910).
Good Sir Palamedes (Wieland & Co., 1912).
The Stratagem (The Mandrake Press, n.d).
Moonchild—A Prologue (The Mandrake Press, 1929).
Diary of a Drug Fiend (Sphere, 1972).
Magick: In Theory and Practice (Castle Books, n.d).
The Magical Record of the Beast 666: The Journals of Aleister Crowley ed. John Symonds and Kenneth Grant (Duckworth, 1972).
The Book of Thoth: A Short Essay on the Tarot, The Equinox, vol. III, no. V. (Samuel Weiser, 1972).
The Qabalah of Aleister Crowley (Samuel Weiser, 1973).
The Equinox, 10 vols. (Samuel Weiser, 1973).
Magick Without Tears, ed. Israel Regardie, (Llewellyn Publications, 1973).
Gems From The Equinox, ed. Israel Regardie, (Llewellyn Publications, 1974).
Crowley On Christ, ed. Francis King, (C. W. Daniel, 1974).
The Complete Astrological Writings, ed. John Symonds and Kenneth Grant (Duckworth, 1974).
Magical and Philosophical Commentaries on The Book of the Law, ed. John Symonds and Kenneth Grant, (93 Publishing, Canada, 1974).
The Law is for All, ed. Israel Regardie (Llewellyn Publications, 1975).
Tao Teh King, ed. Stephen Skinner (Askin Publishers, Ltd., London; Samuel Weiser, 1976).
Seven Seven Seven (Metaphysical Research Group, Hastings, Sussex, 1977).

The Magical Diaries of Aleister Crowley, ed. Stephen Skinner (Neville Spearman, 1979).
Book Four (Samuel Weiser, 1980).
A H A, with Commentary by Israel Regardie (Falcon Press, 1983).

Fuller, Capt. J. F. C.*The Star In The West: A Critical Essay Upon the Works of Aleister Crowley* (Neptune Press, 1976).

Fuller, Jean Overton. *The Magical Dilemma of Victor Neuburg*. (W H Allen, 1965).

Grant, Kenneth. *The Magical Revival* (Frederick Muller, 1972).
——, *Aleister Crowley and the Hidden God* (Frederick Muller, 1973).
——, *Cults of the Shadow* (Frederick Muller, 1975).

Howe, Ellic. *The Magicians of the Golden Dawn* (Routledge & Kegan Paul, 1972; Aquarian Press, 1985).

King, Francis. *Ritual Magic in England: 1887 to the Present Day (Neville Spearman, 1970)*.
——, *Sexuality, Magic and Perversion* (Neville Spearman, 1971).
——, with Stephen Skinner, *Techniques of High Magic* C. W. Daniel, n.d.).
——, *The Secret Rituals of the O.T.O.* (C. W. Daniel, 1973).
——, *The Magical World of Aleister Crowley* (Weidenfeld and Nicolson, 1977).

Lévi, Éliphas *The History of Magic*, translated by A. E. Waite, (Rider & Company, 1957).
——, *Transcendental Magic* (Rider & Company, 1958).

McIntosh, Christopher. *Éliphas Lévi and the French Occult Revival* (Rider & Company, 1972).

Mathers, S. L. MacGregor. *The Kabbalah Unveiled* (Routledge & Kegan Paul, 1951).

Regardie, Israel. *The Golden Dawn, vols. i & ii. An Encyclopedia of Practical Occultism* (Llewellyn Publications; enlarged edition, 1971).
——, *The Golden Dawn, vols. iii & iv* (Llewellyn Publications; enlarged edition, 1971).
——, *The Tree of Life: A Study in Magic* (Thorsons, 1975).
——, *The Eye in the Triangle* (Falcon Press, 1982).

Symonds, John. *The Magic of Aleister Crowley* (Frederick Muller Ltd., 1958).
——, *The Great Beast. The Life and Magick of Aleister Crowley* (Macdonald, 1971).

Index

By the same author:

G.I. GURDJIEFF
The War Against Sleep

The life and work of one of the most influential psychological theorists of the twentieth century

George Ivanovich Gurdjieff is one of the most enigmatic figures of our time. He attracted legends as easily as disciples. But behind the Gurdjieff myth lies a solid corpus of thought, the importance of which is only now being generally recognized. This brilliant and much praised examination of a psychologist and teacher of genius has established itself as the most important and accessible account for the general reader of Gurdjieff's life and work, providing the definitive introduction to the philosophy of Gurdjieff.

G.I. GURDJIEFF: THE WAR AGAINST SLEEP 0 85030 503 9 £6.99 ☐
C.G. JUNG: LORD OF THE UNDERWORLD 0 85030 716 3 £5.99 ☐
NOSTRADAMUS: VISIONS OF THE FUTURE 1 85538 145 1 £5.99 ☐
PAUL BRUNTON: ESSENTIAL READINGS 1 85274 080 9 £7.99 ☐
ROBERT FLUDD: ESSENTIAL READINGS 1 85538 142 7 £9.99 ☐
PARACELSUS: ESSENTIAL READINGS 1 85274 066 3 £7.99 ☐
THE MAGICAL LIFE OF DION FORTUNE 1 85538 051 X £7.99 ☐

All these books are available at your local bookseller or can be ordered direct from the publishers.

To order direct just tick the titles you want and fill in the form below:

Name: _____

Address: _____

_____

_____ _____ Post Code: _____

Send to: Thorsons Mail Order, Dept 32B, HarperCollins*Publishers*, Westerhill Road, Bishopbriggs, Glasgow G64 2QT.
Please enclose a cheque or postal order or your authority to debit your Visa/Access account —

Credit card no: _____

Expiry date: _____

Signature: _____

— to the value of the cover price plus:
UK & BFPO: Add £1.00 for the first book and 25p for each additional book ordered.
Overseas orders including Eire: Please add £2.95 service charge. Books will be sent by surface mail but quotes for airmail despatches will be given on request.

24 HOUR TELEPHONE ORDERING SERVICE FOR ACCESS/VISA CARDHOLDERS — TEL: **041 772 2281.**